GEORGE MULLER'S SERMONS AND ADDRESSES

By

George Muller

BRISTOL

W. F. Mack & Co., 52 Park Row
LONDON:

S. W. PARTRIDGE & CO., 8 and 9, Paternoster Row;
THE BOOK SOCIETY, 28, Paternoster Row.

For hundreds of other excellent titles see:

www.*Classic Christian*Ebooks.com

Inspiring and uplifting classics from authors such as:

E. M. Bounds
Amy Carmichael
Alfred Edersheim
Jonathan Edwards
Charles Finney
D. L. Moody
G. Campbell Morgan
Andrew Murray
Charles Spurgeon
Hudson Taylor
R. A. Torrey
John Wesley

…and many more!

TABLE OF CONTENTS:

Chapter 1: The Twenty-third Psalm. 5
Chapter 2: Yet I will Rejoice in the Lord. 12
Chapter 3: The Lord's Prayer. 17
Chapter 4: The Beloved of the Lamb. 25
Chapter 5: Naaman and Gehazi. 33
Chapter 6: Underneath are the Everlasting Arms. 41
Chapter 7: The Lost Sheep, The Lost Silver, The Prodigal Son. 46
Chapter 8: To Save Sinners. 54
Chapter 9: The Resurrection of the Body. 60
Chapter 10: New Year's Address to Christians. 65
Chapter 11: "The God of all grace…make you perfect" 73
Chapter 12: "Trust in the Lord." 78
Chapter 13: "He was wounded for our transgressions." 87
Chapter 14: Paul's Thorn in the Flesh. 95
Chapter 15: Glorying in the Cross of Christ. 102
Chapter 16: "Open thy mouth wide, and I will fill it." 109
Chapter 17: Christ, the Refuge of Sinners! 118
Chapter 18: The Glad Tidings 125
Chapter 19: Spiritual Building. 131
Chapter 20: "Behold! What Manner of Love." 138

Chapter 1: The Twenty-third Psalm.

A Sermon preached at Bethesda Chapel, Great George Street, Bristol, on Sunday Evening, June 20th, 1897 - Jubilee Sunday.

OUR MEDITATION THIS evening, as the Lord may help us, will be on the short but precious 23rd Psalm, "The Lord is my Shepherd; I shall not want." This was spoken and written by King David. Now, naturally, we should be inclined to say, "No wonder that he said, 'I shall not want,' because he, who had once been a poor shepherd boy, looking after a few sheep, was now a king." And not merely a king, but an exceedingly mighty king, for he had it in his power, if it had been necessary, to send many thousands of soldiers into the battle. And not merely a very mighty king, but an exceedingly rich king. Therefore, we are inclined, naturally, to say, "That was the reason why he said, 'I shall not want.'" He was, indeed, exceedingly rich, for he had gathered together for the building of the Temple such an enormous sum that it would amount to more than 900 millions of pounds sterling of our money! So vast a sum that all the enormous national debt of Great Britain could be cleared off at once by it! And out of his own privy purse alone he had given for the building of the Temple more than 18 million pounds sterling, a thing that has never been since heard of in history.

Yet these were not reasons why he said, "I shall not want," but because Jehovah was his Shepherd! He looked after him. He cared for him. He fed him. He nourished him. And thus the great point regarding ourselves is, that the Lord Jesus is our Shepherd, that we are His sheep; and this we know if we are heeding His voice. Let us ask ourselves, Do we hear the voice of the Lord Jesus? Do we attend to what He says? Are we mindful of seeking to please Him, and to carry out His Word in Our life and deportment? And, above all, do we trust in Him Who laid down His life for the sheep, Who made an atonement for poor sinners, whereby all who trust in Him for salvation might be saved? These are deeply important questions, which we should aim to be able to answer in the affirmative Thus it is with me. Then, even though we may be amongst the poorest, the most ignorant, the most tried persons on earth, we, too, shall be warranted by the fact that we are the sheep of Christ to say, "I shall no want."

And here particularly notice this. "I shall not want" does not simply refer to bodily necessities, nor merely to mental necessities, but to everything that we can possibly need while here on earth. If we find the spiritual conflict is great, and we seek more and more to enter into our weakness, and helplessness, and nothingness, and entire dependence on God for assistance, here is a word for our comfort which does not belong to David only, but to us also, individually, if we have Jehovah-Jesus for our Shepherd. In whatever want, of whatever kind, we possibly can be while on the road to Heaven, it is our precious, glorious privilege, with David, to say to ourselves, "I shall not want, because my Heavenly Father is my Shepherd, my precious adorable Lord Jesus Christ is my Helper, my Friend, my Elder Brother, my Saviour. He will never leave me, nor forsake me!" O, how unspeakably blessed is the position of the weakest, the feeblest, the least instructed child of God! Therefore the great, the deeply important question once more is this, "Do we belong, individually, to the sheep of Christ?" My heart's desire and prayer is that everyone here present may with earnestness seek to get into such a Scriptural state of heart, as to be warranted to say, "The Lord is my Shepherd, I shall not want."

In the second verse, the figure of the shepherd and the sheep is kept up. "He maketh me to lie down in green pastures." Not "driveth me to a few dry blades of grass." But green pastures, tender grass. Then, the sheep are not driven to these; but they are at leisure to partake of the green grass, the tender grass, the "green pastures," and to lie down and to rise again, as sheep. Now, the figures here used bring before us the blessedness of a child of God! The world knows nothing of our happiness in the Lord, and cannot, therefore, in the least degree enter into the blessedness of our position as God's children.

Our eyes have been opened to see the awful state in which we are by nature; that is, led captive by the devil, at his will, to do the things which are hateful to God and perfectly contrary to His mind. Further, it has pleased the Lord not merely to show to us this lost and ruined condition, but to enable us to own it before Him, to confess that we are undone, lost, and ruined, and that we cannot save ourselves. Even this is not all. But God has helped us by the power of His Holy Spirit to put our trust simply, solely, and entirely in what the Lord Jesus Christ has done for sinners, even fulfilling the whole law of God in our room and stead, and bearing the punishment which we have deserved on account of our numberless transgressions, so that we stand before God as just ones. That means we are reckoned on the part of God as just and righteous--unjust and unrighteous though we are in ourselves. We, through this faith in the Lord Jesus Christ, not merely become children of God, and heirs of God, and joint-heirs with Christ; but already, while yet in the body, all our numberless transgressions are forgiven.

We have not to wait till we die, or till the Lord Jesus Christ comes, in order to obtain forgiveness from all our sins; but the moment we put our trust alone in Jesus for salvation, that moment every one of our numberless transgressions is forgiven, and shall be remembered no more throughout eternity. O, how unspeakably blessed is this position, and the result of it is peace and joy in the Holy Ghost! We, without dread and fear, now think about God-so to speak, look Him in the face, guilty sinners though we are naturally-without being in the least afraid of an eternally Holy God. O, how precious! How unspeakably precious this is!

And then, when at last it pleases God to take us home to Himself, after He has helped us during the whole of our earthly pilgrimage, in all our variety of difficulties, and trials, and perplexing circumstances, and amid the manifestations of our weakness and helplessness-when at last He takes us to Himself, either by passing through death, or, if found alive at the return of the Lord Jesus Christ, being taken to Him, then we enter upon our inheritance. And that inheritance is nothing less than what our Heavenly Father gives to His Only Begotten Son, as the reward of His mediatorial service, for all He did on earth, for all He suffered on earth, for the passing through the hour of darkness, in order that the innumerable company of poor sinners which no man is able to count might be saved.

What our Heavenly Father gives to Him in the way of glory and reward for all this, we who put our trust in Him shall share with Him. We can say to ourselves, as believers in the Lord Jesus, "Though I deserve nothing but hell, I shall not only have Heaven, I shall not only partake of the rivers of pleasure at the right hand of God, but I shall share with my precious adorable Lord Jesus Christ all the glory which the Father gives to Him for His mediatorial work!" O, what is contained in this! If the world only knew what the sinner who believes in Christ obtains through faith in Him, all the world would joyfully seek Him; but it is because it is not apprehended, it is not known, that with carelessness and indifference the world passes on, and often and often till it is too late to awake it.

"He maketh me to lie down in green pastures." The figure here used regarding the sheep brings before us the exceeding great blessings and happiness which are the result of putting our trust in the Lord Jesus Christ. What, therefore, we have to do is to seek more and more to ponder it, and more and more to enter into it, with reference to ourselves. Then, not merely "green pastures" are mentioned, but "still waters." "He leadeth me beside the still waters;" the waters of quietness, on account of the timid nature of the sheep. This is especially referred to. Not a mountain torrent, which might frighten away the sheep, are they led to for drinking; but to the quiet still waters, in character with the sheep. They are not frightened away. "He restoreth my soul; He leadeth me in the paths of righteousness, for His Name's sake." I will mention here (what I have mentioned, I think, before) that this has nothing to do with bringing backsliders to Himself again. In the Hebrew, the words mean, "He refresheth my soul," or "He invigorates my soul; " just as by means of a very good night's rest we are invigorated and refreshed, or as a cooling draught of water given at the time of harvest on a hot summer's day to the labourer would refresh him, so, spiritually, we, who are the children of God, are refreshed by our Precious Shepherd.

It is the very joy and delight of the heart of our precious Lord Jesus Christ to refresh us spiritually. If at any time we are cast down, through trials and difficulties, or through sore temptations, which we have to encounter, and we find that we are not being refreshed, what we should do is to remind the Lord Jesus Christ that to Him "hath been given the tongue of the learned, that He might know how to speak a word in season to them that are weary," to them who have need to be refreshed, to comfort them; to encourage them, to strengthen their hands in God. This precious word we have brought before us regarding the Lord Jesus Christ in the 4th verse of the 50th chapter of Isaiah, and I advise all my beloved brethren and sisters in Christ to make much more use than they have yet done of this blessed word.

"He refresheth my soul." O let us make use of this! O let us, in childlike simplicity, trust our precious, precious Lord Jesus Christ! Whenever you are cast down, whenever you are greatly tried spiritually, open your heart to the precious Jesus, as your Friend. I have done it for many a long year, and it is just this which upholds me, which comforts me, which makes me a happy man. I deal with my precious Lord Jesus as a bosom Friend. I pour out my whole heart to Him, and tell Him all, everything; and beg and intreat Him, whenever I need it, to speak to me a word in season, that the weariness may pass away, and that I may be refreshed spiritually. And I find Him ever ready to help me. "He restoreth my soul; He leadeth me in the paths of righteousness, for His Name's sake." The Lord brings us into the right road, into "the paths of righteousness," and we are depending on Him to be led along in the same road, for we should soon wander away from Him and go back again to our own foolish, sinful desires. This second part of the verse shows what is meant by "He restoreth my soul;" that is, "He refresheth my soul, He leads me along in the right road."

"Yea, though I walk through the valley of the shadow of death, I will fear no evil, for Thou art with me; Thy rod and Thy staff, they comfort me." Here we find the Psalmist supposing himself to be brought to meet the greatest trial, the greatest affliction; nay, to be brought to the very close of life, to pass through the ordeal of death. Yet his language is, "Though I walk through the valley of the shadow of death, I will fear no evil." How comes this? Is it because we have so much medical power? Surely not! When we are brought to the very brink of the grave, is it because we have so much physical power and strength? No! But quite the reverse. The reason is this: because we have the Lord Jesus with us! "Though I walk through the valley of the shadow of death, I will fear no evil, for Thou art with me." O how precious! The Lord caring for us, by His passing with us through the Vale of Tears.

When we are brought to the condition that more than ever we need Him, as a Friend, as a Helper, as a Support, there He is, never leaving us, nor forsaking us! What we have to say individually to ourselves when the heaviest and greatest trials come, and when we are brought even to the very brink of the grave, and when heart and flesh fail, is, "Thou art with me; Thou, my precious Lord Jesus, art with me; Thou hast not forsaken me, Thou art now with me, in my utter weakness and helplessness; I have Thee as my Almighty Friend and Upholder, and Comforter and Strength." O how precious! "Yea, though I walk through the valley of the shadow of death, I will fear no evil." Some of the dear children of God, the real, true children of God, have fear regarding the hour of death. "How will it be when I come to die?" they think. O say to yourself, "I will fear no evil!" Not because we are anything in ourselves, or can do anything by ourselves; but simply because it is written, "Thou art with me; Thy rod and Thy staff, they comfort me."

Now the last two verses place before us the intimate connection between God and His children, under another figure-under the figure of a host inviting guests. "Thou preparest a table before me, in the presence of mine enemies; Thou anointest my head with oil; my cup runneth over." Taking this verse, what is the meaning? It consists in two things. Trusting the Lord Jesus Christ, the one on whom we have to feed; seeking to enter into what God has given us in Jesus Christ, as the Law Fulfiller, as the Atoner for our sins, and on Whom we have to feed spiritually. That is the table which God has prepared for us. Secondly, the Word of God, the revealed Will of God, as we have it in the Holy Scriptures, that is what God gives to us for our food; and this notwithstanding all the hatred of Satan, notwithstanding all the opposition of our enemies. "Thou preparest a table before me, in the presence of mine enemies."

But now comes the practical question, "Do we feed practically on Christ? Do we seek at large to ponder what the Lord Jesus Christ is to us, as our Redeemer, as our Great High Priest, as the one who is coming again to take us to Himself, that where He is we may be also? What the Lord Jesus Christ is to us as our Friend, as our Counsellor, as our Strength? Now do we seek in Him an interest, and do we day by day put on (to use the figure that is used in Scripture) the helmet of our salvation; that is, seek to enter into what is connected with the return of the Lord Jesus Christ? Do we comfort ourselves day by day with all this?" O how deeply important to attend to it that we may have peace and joy in the Holy Ghost, that the world may see what a blessed thing it is to be a child of God-that thus we may not only glorify Him, but strengthen the hands of our fellow-men.

"Thou anointest my head with oil; my cup runneth over." In the east, when a great one invited anyone of his friends to take a meal with him, to spend a day with him, one of the first things was not only that the servants should hand him water to wash his feet, but oil to anoint his head. As a mark of respect and reverence this was done. That was the welcome, so to speak, given to the guest who came to the house of the great one. Now, we have no such thing done to us, but something infinitely more precious. The Holy Spirit is given to us-the Holy Spirit again and again represented under the figure of oil. And as assuredly as we have the Holy Ghost given to us, so surely shall we get to Heaven, so surely shall we share the glory of Christ, so surely shall we become like Christ and have our glorified bodies. These are the things which are implied in the gift of the Holy Spirit! O how precious these things are!

If the heart habitually were given to these things, it would be full of joy! We should be exceedingly happy; and therefore my affectionate counsel and advice to my beloved fellow-believers is, seek more and more to ponder all this, with application to your own hearts, in order that your joy may increase more abundantly. And what will come of it at last? You will be able to say with the Psalmist, "My cup runneth over"-"I am so happy a man that I can scarcely bear it; I not only have something in my cup, and a good deal in my cup, and have my cup full; but my cup runneth over." O the blessed position of a child of God, not as to pounds, shillings, and pence, not as to the possession of many houses, not as to the possession of a great many hundreds of acres of land, not because he has an enormous sum in the Funds-not on these accounts. There may be little, or nothing at all, of all this found in his possession. But as to peace and joy in the Holy Ghost, as to the blessedness of having this brought down into his heart. O, my friends, how precious this!

Now comes the last verse, "Surely goodness and mercy shall follow me all the days of my life, and I will dwell in the house of the Lord forever." The poor one has been invited as a guest by the Rich One. He goes, and finds it very pleasant there, and is happy. All that is just what he desires naturally. Now, what conclusion does he come to? "I find it so very pleasant to be here, I will remain here, I will not go away any more." This brings before us what the child of God finds, in acquaintance with Christ. Not merely entering into what God has given him in Christ Jesus; not merely having to say, "My cup runneth over; I am brimful of happiness." But, "I have almost more than I can bear. I find it so pleasant, so exceedingly pleasant, this way of going on, I can never get into another position any more. I will remain in the house of my Heavenly Father forever."

That is the position into which we are brought as believers in Christ! And as assuredly as we are honestly walking in the ways of the Lord, and truly surrendering the heart to God, this is the result to which we come. We find it so pleasant, so precious, even for this life, that we have no desire to depart from the ways of the Lord. In our natural, worldly condition, we seek after happiness; but we do not get it. Nothing but disappointment is the result, for after a few hours all this worldly happiness is gone. But the position in which we are brought by faith in the Lord Jesus Christ not only insures us happiness for a few days, or a few months, or a few years, but for ever and ever. So that our heart says, "I will remain in this way; I am so happy in this way; I will never forsake this way."

Not merely so. But "Goodness and mercy shall follow me all the days of my life.' I shall now be for ever and ever a happy man, and I will remain in the presence of my Father; I will not leave His House anymore, because I have found it so very, very precious to be a child of God." Now, this has been my own happy experience for seventy-one years and a half, and therefore I commend this plan, which is according to the Holy Scriptures, to any and everyone who has not yet had it. It is not merely for this one, or another one; but God is willing to bestow the blessing upon any and everyone who is desirous of having it. All we have to do is, just like mere beggars, to open our hands and to receive what God is willing to give to us. We have to own that we deserve nothing but punishment; we have to own that we are sinners who, on account of our natural sinfulness, are entirely unworthy of all the blessings which God is willing to bestow upon us; and owning to this, and then putting our trust in the Lord Jesus Christ for salvation, ensures to us these gifts.

Will you not accept them if you have not accepted them yet? Will you all who have not yet put your trust in Jesus, do so now? O what unspeakable blessedness is here! I remember well the very first evening after my conversion lying peacefully on my bed, knowing that my sins were forgiven, that Heaven was my Home, that I was now regenerated, brought on the road to Heaven, and my heart was ready to leap for joy. And ever since matters have gone on in the same way, and this is the blessedness I desire for everyone who is yet without it. God give the blessing, and abundant blessing, for Christ's sake.

Chapter 2: Yet I will Rejoice in the Lord.

A Sermon preached at Bethesda Chapel, Great George Street, Bristol, on Sunday Evening; June 13th, 1897.

Habakkuk 3: 17-19.

IN THE FIRST verse under notice we have brought before us not merely the loss of one thing, or of another thing, or of anything, but the loss on the part of the Jew of everything, for they were in an agricultural country generally speaking; and the prophet Habakkuk says regarding himself, "Although the fig tree shall not blossom, neither shall fruit be in the vines, the labour of the olive shall fail, and the fields shall yield no meat, the flocks shall be cut off from the fold, and there shall be no herd in the stalls, yet I will rejoice in the Lord, I will joy in the God of my salvation." Now, this is the great and deeply important question, What is it that brought this man of God to the decision that though he should lose everything, though he should be reduced to a state of the greatest poverty and difficulty and affliction, yet he would rejoice in Jehovah? What was it that brought him to this? Because the Living God has given Himself to every one of His children as their portion! He has given Himself to every one of His children, so that whatever they may lose, in regard to the things connected with this life, God remains to them; in other words, their ALL remains to them. They are not, and they never really and truly can be, losers of anything that is worth anything, for God remains.

He gives Himself to every one of His children, to the weakest, the feeblest, the least instructed among them, as their portion; therefore, having Him, they have everything they could wish. God remains to them; He gives Himself to His children, once for all; they have, once for all, blessing to make them happy; they have, once for all, kindness, mercy, and grace, bestowed on them, sufficient for their whole earthly pilgrimage, and for the whole of eternity. O beloved in Christ, and O beloved ones who are not yet believers in Christ, let us all really and truly seek to enter into what it is to have God, and what it means that God gives Himself to us. Two verses of the 73rd Psalm and many similar portions might be brought to bear, but I think these two verses will do, "Whom have I in Heaven but Thee? And there is none upon earth that I desire beside Thee. My flesh and my heart faileth." The Psalmist supposes himself to be brought to the end of his earthly pilgrimage, brought to the point of death. "My flesh and my heart faileth, but God is the strength of my heart, and my portion forever." God had been his portion in life, and now he was going out of time into eternity, God remains his portion Not only for a few years, or for a few hundred years, but for ever God remains true to His people. If this were entered into what happy persons we should be! O, if only held on to by faith and realised, what peace and joy in the Holy Ghost we should have-- not merely now and then, not merely frequently, but habitually! O, how exceedingly precious! God gives Himself, and with all He is and has to the weakest, the feeblest of His children. O, how precious! How exceedingly precious!

And the prophet Habakkuk entered into it, and it was just this that made him so happy. Though he should lose everything that this world could give, yet would he rejoice in Jehovah. "Yet, I will rejoice in the Lord"- it means Jehovah-"I will joy in the God of my salvation." Now, let us just for a little while ponder somewhat more minutely what we have here, what we receive from God as poor sinners, trusting in the Lord Jesus Christ; and what other poor sinners might have if they were only willing to know what God is prepared to give to those who come to Him through Jesus Christ. First of all, He opens our eyes and shows to us the lost and ruined condition in which we are by nature; makes manifest our complete spiritual darkness and ignorance. He further shows to us that we cannot save ourselves, that salvation entirely depends on Himself, through the gift of His Only Begotten Son, Whose perfect obedience unto death He accepts in our room and stead. Now, all this is in the first place to be seen, to be apprehended, to be laid hold on by faith, in order that our eyes, being opened, we may have the beginning of peace and joy. Further, so far even as this present life is concerned, we at once, through faith in the Lord Jesus, obtain full forgiveness for all our numberless transgressions. We are accepted in the beloved, in Jesus Christ, and treated as righteous ones, as just ones, though in ourselves unjust ones and unrighteous ones. So accepted in the beloved, and treated as justified ones, accepted in the beloved and treated as forgiven ones, not one single transgression shall be mentioned against us any more. All, all is forgiven! Entering into it oh, what peace it gives to the soul, entering into it more and more it brings joy in God; the heart is filled with gratitude to Him for what He has done for us in Jesus Christ. But what I have mentioned is not all. We thus being born again, regenerated, obtain spiritual life; while before we were dead in trespasses and sins. Now, through faith in the Lord Jesus Christ, we obtain spiritual life; that life is everlasting. The beginning of this everlasting life is made when we are brought to believe in Jesus, and this spiritual life is continued, this spiritual life lasts, when the natural life is come to an end, when we pass out of time into Eternity. This is another blessing. Then we are now, through this faith in the Lord Jesus Christ, the children of God not merely in name, but in reality. We have obtained spiritual life. We are born again by the power of God's Holy Spirit. We are really and truly the children of God, and as such we are really and truly heirs of God, and joint-heirs with the Lord Jesus Christ; and thus we have everything that we could possibly wish. We are infinitely rich as the children of God, as the heirs of God, as the joint-heirs with the Lord Jesus, for we partake of all the things which the Father gives to Him, as a recompense for His mediatorial work on earth. Thus we not only become infinitely rich, but we are infinitely honoured, for we share the honour which the Father bestows upon His only begotten Son as the reward for His great work. Oh, what an abounding reason, therefore, we have to rejoice in the Lord, in Jehovah!

Being in this state, whatever may be our difficulties, our trials, our necessities, we can obtain help from God, because we are the children whom He loves with an eternal, unchangeable love-the children who are so dear to His heart that they are precious in His sight, and loved by Him even as He loves His only begotten Son, for they belong to Christ, they are members of that mystical body of which He is the Head. What, therefore, can they possibly want that they cannot receive? Their God and Father in Christ Jesus is willing to impart to everyone of them, even the feeblest and weakest among them, every blessing that really would be a blessing to them, everything that really would be for their good and profit, and, therefore, to the glory of God. In the midst of trials and temptations, sore temptations, great attacks of Satan, we may come to Him, in our utter weakness and helplessness, and nothingness, and ask Him to fight our battles for us, to help us, to stand at our side, to rebuke the wicked one, and to drive him from us. All this our Heavenly Father delights to do, because He loves us so dearly and tenderly. He loves us with an eternal unchangeable love. He loves us as He loves His only begotten Son. Oh, how precious is all this!

Now notice further the title that is given to God. He is called in the 18th verse, "The God of my salvation." He is the God of salvation; but the preciousness of the statement lies in this, that we have proved Him to ourselves thus, and are able to say, "The God of my salvation." That is just the language of my heart! Now, how many of us are able to say this? I say, "He is the God of my salvation." I glory in it, I rejoice in it, for, by the grace of God, I am as certain that I shall go to Heaven as if I were there already! Therefore, I say, "He is the God of my salvation." And there are many scores here present who, like myself, can say and sing, "He is the God of my salvation." But if there are any here who are not yet able to say this, give yourselves no rest till you can. First of all, you must come to see that you are sinners needing salvation. If you do not see it, ask God to show it to you, and, as a means to come to the knowledge of it, read carefully three or four times the first three chapters of the Epistle of Paul to the Romans, and the second chapter of the Epistle of Paul to the Ephesians. Read these portions with application to yourselves, and if still you do not see that you are sinners needing a Saviour, read yet again these very portions, and ask God to open your eyes. Then, when you see what is contained therein, ask

God to help you to put your trust in Jesus for salvation, for He in our room fulfilled the law of God, and, therefore, sets us free, and He in our room and stead bore the punishment due to us.

When able to apprehend this, we no longer dread God; we are no longer afraid of God, but look on Him as our Father, as our Friend, as our Helper Who has loved us in Christ Jesus. But if yet we have no peace in our souls, let us go on asking God that we may, by the power of His Holy Spirit, apprehend more feelingly and truly the work of Christ, and to enter into it that we may have that full peace and joy, which God delights to give to everyone of His children. "Although the fig tree shall not blossom, neither shall fruit be in the vines, the labour of the olive shall fail, and the fields shall yield no meat, the flock shall be cut off from the fold, and there shall be no herd in the stalls, yet, I will rejoice in Jehovah, I will joy in the God of my salvation." Oh, if any of you know this, how greatly are you blessed! Oh, if everyone here knew this what an encouragement it would be to sinners who have not yet obtained this peace and joy in God!

Now we come to the last verse, "The Lord God is my strength, and He will make my feet like hinds' feet, and He will make me to walk upon mine high places." "The Lord God," that is Jehovah-for you know that whenever we have the word "Lord" printed in large characters, it invariably means this, "Jehovah"- "is my strength." Was he weak physically? God would be able to strengthen him, for He was his strength! Was he weak spiritually, amid temptations, great and varied and many, and of a lasting character? Jehovah was his strength; therefore, what could he lack? Was he poor in any way? Did he require anything for the life that now is? Or, for himself, or for his family, or under any circumstances, did he require anything which would be for the glory of God? God was able and willing to communicate it to him! Now that is just what we have to lay hold of, that Jehovah is the strength of His children physically, mentally, spiritually; and this not now and then, but at all times and under all circumstances, however great the power of our spiritual adversaries may be, and however fearfully they may attack us in order to overcome us, " God is my strength, and He will make my feet like hinds' feet, and He will make me to walk upon mine high places." The feet like a roe, a wild animal running. For what? To act according to the mind of God! That, I judge, is particularly meant here by the words, "He will make my feet like hinds' feet" Not to accomplish our own purposes, not to enjoy ourselves, but to act according to the mind of God! The will of God presented to us, and instantaneously and with the greatest alacrity acted upon; therefore, the words, "hinds' feet," means that no delay is made, but immediately the will of God is carried out.

Then one other point. "He will make me to walk upon mine high places." The heart of the prophet Habakkuk was in Heaven, and he looked down on the things here below, and the state in which he was. O to enter into it, though we are poor sinners, that we are seated with Christ in heavenly places! That, therefore, we should treat all human affairs as those who are seated in Heaven in Christ Jesus, and look down from Heaven, so to speak, on the poor, weak, feeble, earthly affairs here below, and judge about them as those who are already in glory, who are already in Heaven.

Now, if one or the other says, "But I am yet in the body; I find a difficulty thus to think, to judge, and to act," my reply is, "So do I, but the grace of God can bring us to this state."

"He will make me to walk upon mine high places." These high places are those in which his heart is fixed, and this is just what we individually should have-*the heart in Heaven*. While in the body, we must attend to the affairs of this life; God would not have us give up our earthly occupations because of the difficulties connected with these things. But we must yet remain in the position to which God has brought us, entering into the spiritual life which has been given to us, remembering that this spiritual life is eternal, that more and more it will be developed, and that at last it will come to the full fruition and we shall be holy, as our Lord Jesus Christ was holy while on earth and as He ever has been since He ascended to Heaven, and that we shall at the same time have a glorified body, as the Lord Jesus Christ had when He was raised from the dead. These are the blessed prospects of the weakest and feeblest child of God!

Oh, what a precious blessing has God bestowed on us in Christ Jesus! Oh, what are we poor miserable sinners come to by faith in Him! Our great business, therefore, must be in child-like simplicity to ponder all the wondrous blessings God has bestowed on us through His Son, and, in child-like simplicity, to believe everything that He has declared regarding us as believers in the Lord Jesus Christ, and in joyful anticipation look forward to the day when all this will have its complete accomplishment, when we shall no longer walk by faith, but by sight, having everyone of these blessings in actual possession. Now, one word more. Are there any here present who up to this time have been thoughtlessly and carelessly unconcerned about the things of God? If so, I now entreat and beseech you no longer to be thus-for the salvation of your souls, your happiness here, and throughout Eternity, depend upon your receiving Christ. Salvation is also to be had by faith in Jesus Christ, and God is willing to bestow the blessing on every and anyone, however great and many their transgressions may be. Only let them own that they are sinners, deserving nothing but punishment, and only let them put their trust in Jesus, and the blessing is theirs forever.

Chapter 3: The Lord's Prayer.

A Sermon preached at Bethesda Chapel, Great George Street, Bristol, on Sunday Evening, March 21st, 1897.

Matthew 6:5-15.

WE WILL MEDITATE on part of Matthew 6, commencing at verse 5: "When thou prayest, thou shalt not be as the hypocrites are, for they love to pray standing in the synagogues, and in the corners of the streets, that they may be seen of men. Verily, I say unto you, they have their reward." In reference to not a few of the Pharisees of old this was actually the case. They would stand for a long time in the synagogues praying; but what was far worse than this, when the ordinary prayer time came for the Israelites-about three o'clock in the afternoon by our time-they would so manage it that just at that very time they could be found at the corners of the streets, where they might be observed in the act of prayer by as many as possible coming from various directions. All this was hypocrisy. They professed thus to be very holy men, but in reality it was the reverse. "Verily, I say unto you, they have their reward." Their reward was the applause of their fellow-men. A poor, miserable recompense.

"But when thou prayest, enter into thy closet." The great point here is the secrecy in reference to prayer. Not all persons are in such a position as that they have a little chamber to which they can retire and lock the door. But if it can be done, it should be done. If impossible, God will accept according to our position and circumstances. I remember a case which I would relate to show how persons may be situated. About 50 years ago I went to Germany to find missionaries for the East Indies. On this journey I came to Magdeburg, one of the strongest and largest fortresses of the kingdom of Prussia. Here I found in the house of a godly man in the Army a comrade of his, and, as he lived in barracks, I said, My dear brother, how do you manage with regard to prayer, as you are continually surrounded by hundreds of soldiers?" His reply was, "When I want to pray in secret, I go down into a large sand-cellar, which is perfectly dark, and there I kneel down on the sand. No one is able to see I am there, though often some of my comrades come close to my heels; but never am I found there. I am alone, perfectly alone; no one sees me; and that is my closet." So in whatever variety of ways the children of God may be situated, they have to do the best they can. But the great point is that as much as possible we should seek to deal with our Heavenly Father in the way of prayer in secret; and under no circumstances aim to be noticed by our fellow-men in order to get their applause.

"When thou prayest, enter into thy closet, and when thou hast shut thy door" (thus further stating the exceeding great importance of secrecy). "Pray to thy Father which is in secret, and thy Father, which seeth in secret, shall reward thee openly." Where there is this, a secret waiting on God, He, in His Own time and way, will give the open recompense. He will show that He is noticing; He will show that He has recorded it in the book of remembrance; He will show that it has not escaped His observation. "Thy Father which seeth in secret, shall reward thee openly." The secret waiting on God will be manifested by blessing. As assuredly as we thus give ourselves to prayer, God will notice us, and give blessing, that anyone can see.

"But when ye pray, use not vain repetitions, as the heathen do." That is, sentence by sentence, repeating the same request, just as Baal's worshippers did, and as the heathen nations do up to the present time, thinking that the more their words, the more the repetition of what they ask for, the more certain is it that they will get it. "Use not vain repetitions as the heathen do, for they think that they shall be heard for their much speaking; be not ye, therefore, like unto them, for your Father knoweth what things ye have need of, before ye ask Him." Prayer is not necessary for the sake of informing God; but prayer is necessary simply because it is the appointment of God. He will have us go to Him for our own good and profit and blessing, asking Him for the things we require, because the blessing bestowed on us in answer to prayer is so much the more precious than if the blessing were given without prayer. Often and often God allows us greatly to be tried, in order that at last, when the blessing does come and prayer is answered, it may be all the more precious to us "Be not ye, therefore, like unto them, for your Father knoweth what things ye have need of, before ye ask Him."

Now comes what is commonly called, "The Lord's Prayer." After this manner, therefore, pray ye." This shows us it is not God's appointment that these words of the Lord Jesus Christ should only be used, nor that we should continually use them. But in the spirit, in this manner we should ask blessing. That is the lesson we have to learn. "After this manner pray ye, 'Our Father, which art in Heaven.'" The very first word is full of meaning. The petitions which are recorded here are suitable, and only suitable, for the children of God-for they are the prayer of the heavenly family, those who are believers in the Lord Jesus Christ. We have to keep this before us, that as long as we are not believers in the Lord Jesus Christ, God is not our Father. God is God to us. He is our Creator. He is our Preserver. He is the One Who supplies us with everything that we can need. He lets His sun shine for us; He lets the rain fall also, so that we are benefited by it. But until we are believers in the Lord Jesus Christ, God is not our Father. Now this word "Our," shows that we are part of a family, part of the heavenly family; and thus it is that all who put their trust in the Lord Jesus Christ for the salvation of their souls, after having been convinced that they are sinners, deserving nothing but punishment-all such as are believers-have in God Almighty a Father. "Who art in Heaven." His place is everywhere; but especially is it in Heaven, not on earth, though His power may be seen everywhere, and the manifestations of His presence be found throughout the universe.

"Hallowed by Thy Name." That is, Thy Name be honoured; Thy Name be glorified. And here I remind my beloved Christian friends of the meaning of the word "Name." It does not mean the several letters which form the name of "God," but what we learn in the 34th chapter of Exodus, when Jehovah proclaimed His Name before Moses. It is His Character, His Attributes, what He is Himself, which are to be glorified. Jehovah, the God and Father of our Lord Jesus Christ, the Father of all those who believe in Jesus is to be glorified. That is the meaning of "Hallowed be Thy Name;" and just in the proportion in which we enter into what God is, we find out what a lovely, lovely Being He is, how infinitely lovely He is, "Hallowed be Thy Name." In other words, "I pray that Thou mayest be more and more honoured and glorified."

Now comes another petition. "Thy kingdom come." That is, "Hasten the time, bring it about speedily, when Thou shalt universally be honoured, when Thou shalt universally be glorified, when all the works of the wicked one shall be destroyed." This will be after the return of the Lord Jesus Christ. See how entirely impossible it is for the ungodly, the unconverted, to ask this petition from the heart. The lips of such may utter it times without number, but the true meaning is nothing short of this: "Let the time speedily come when I, a wicked creature, shall be cast into the bottomless pit." That is just the meaning of the prayer when so uttered; and of course this plainly shows that only in ignorance the ungodly could ask the petition, "Thy kingdom come." The words can only properly be used by those who are believers in the Lord Jesus, for they beseech Him soon to return, that God universally may be glorified and honoured by everyone on earth. That this is the meaning we see immediately from what follows.

"Thy will be done in earth, as it is in Heaven." Since the fall of Adam and Eve, the will of God is not done on earth. It was done before the fall of Adam and Eve in Paradise, but from the moment they ate of the forbidden fruit, and sin was introduced by the devil on earth, from that moment the will of God was not done to the full on earth, as it should be, and as it will he hereafter when the Lord Jesus Christ has returned. Let us clearly keep this before us. One of the first things which was done after the fall was that the first child of Adam and Eve, Cain, murdered his own brother, Abel. There we see the fruit of sin entering into the world, and ever since then the will of God has not been "done in earth, as it is in Heaven." There have been those godly in spirit, at various times, who have sought in their feeble measure to glorify God, and to walk to the praise and glory and honour of His Name. But the great mass of human beings on earth have not been doing the will of God, as the will of God is done in Heaven.

"Give us this day our daily bread." Here the daily bread does not mean simply bread and nothing else; but it means the necessaries of life generally. What we require we ask God for, and are allowed to ask God to give to us. Notice, particularly, that it is not stated here, "Give us our daily bread," but "Give us this day our daily bread." That means we are not warranted to expect a great abundance, in the way of supply of earthly things. God may be going to fill our hearts with cause for gratitude; God may most abundantly give to us the necessaries of life beforehand, and a long time beforehand; but if He does not do it, we are not to blame Him, far less to consider He is not faithful to His promise, for He has not promised that He will give us years beforehand, neither months beforehand, neither weeks beforehand, neither many days beforehand, the necessaries of life; but He has only promised that day by day we shall be supplied, and this also only under the condition that we seek first the Kingdom of God, and His Righteousness. In other words, if we walk in the fear of God, making it our business to win souls for Him, and to set a good example of godly walk and behaviour before our fellow-men, we shall then as assuredly as we trust in Him be supplied with the necessaries of life. For so did David say, "I have been young and now am old, yet have I not seen the righteous forsaken, nor his seed "-i.e., his children, his descendants-" begging bread." "Give us this day our daily bread." On this petition we may write clothes, house rent, taxes, supplies for all that which our family requires. All this is implied in the petition for daily bread. And how precious to have to go to a Loving Father, Whose very joy and delight it is to answer the petitions of His children. He is not a hard Master, an austere Being, but an infinitely loving Father. Oh, that increasingly it might come to everyone of the children of God to look at Him as an infinitely loving Being; for when we are brought to this state we are perfectly satisfied at all times, and under all circumstances with His dealings with us. Whether painful or otherwise, we are satisfied that He doeth all things well.

"And forgive us our debts, as we forgive our debtors." This implies the owning that we are sinners. It is a matter of exceeding great importance that we give ourselves to God as we are, not seeking to make out that we are very good people, very excellent people, that we walk habitually in His ways and act according to His Mind-for the very reverse is the case, more or less, with everyone of us even the best among us. Therefore, we should increasingly own before God that we are sinners, that we have not acted at every time and under every circumstance according to His Mind, and have accordingly contracted debts, spiritual debts, because we are transgressors. We should own that we are debtors before God, and ask His forgiveness, for Christ's sake, seeking it in God's appointed way through Jesus. Not on any account seeking forgiveness by pretending henceforth we will live a better life, that we will make up for our misconduct; that can never be done. We can never make up for past transgressions, for moment by moment we are expected to love God, with all our heart, with all our strength, with all our might, and to walk in His ways to the praise of His Name. Therefore we can never by our own doings make up for past misconduct. But, through faith in Jesus, if we put our trust in Him for salvation, the Righteousness of Christ is imputed to us. In other words, the holy work and life of the Lord Jesus is put to our account, as if we had been blameless, as if we had been without sin, as if we had walked as consistently all our days as the precious Jesus did. His righteousness is imputed to us, and by that alone forgiveness is to be obtained-putting our trust in Him, seeing Him hanging on the cross, shedding His blood as the Sinbearer, Who made an atonement for our sins, and through Whom alone we can obtain reconciliation.

"As we forgive our debtors." This is particularly to be noticed. If anyone has offended us, transgressed against us, behaved improperly towards us, are we ready to forgive? Are we habitually forgiving? Even if it should occur many times, yet if the individual who offends us, and behaves improperly towards us, makes confession, we are to be ready to forgive, and, supposing this to be done, it is stated, "As we forgive our debtors." Here I would particularly mention that we are not warranted to expect answers to our prayers if we are not acting according to this. I judge that this often and often is a hindrance to obtaining answers to our prayers, because we cultivate an unforgiving spirit, we are not ready to forgive those who have offended us and behaved improperly toward us. "Forgive us our debts, as we forgive our debtors," that should be true of us.

"And lead us not into temptation, but deliver us from evil." Our weakness, our helplessness, our nothingness remain, as long as we are in the body, and we shall be liable to temptation, and exposed to temptation. The Lord Jesus Christ found this. It may be in our case, as it was with Him, that for a season the tempter leaves us. For a season he may not specially seek to overpower us, but it will be only for a season, he will come again. That, however, is only one side of the truth; and the other side of the truth is this, that God is ready to succour and help His children. All through their pilgrimage, if they only own their weakness and come to Him and seek His assistance, He is ready to help. Our prayer, therefore, is to be this; that God, in the riches of His grace, would allow us no more to be tempted than is absolutely needful for the glory of His Name, and to become more and more acquainted with His power, with His love, and His readiness to appear on our behalf.

Then it is added, "But deliver us from evil." That more especially means the devil himself; "from the evil one, the wicked one, deliver us." For it is he who is the source of evil, and the greatest evil, since it is he who has such craftiness, and is continually ready to get an advantage over us. Therefore, above all, our prayer should be this: "Deliver us from the wicked one, the evil one, the devil; allow him not to get an advantage over us;" and this prayer is to be uttered from the heart, to the very last moment of our earthly pilgrimage. We never get into that state that we are so perfectly holy, so perfectly sinless, so perfectly Christ-like, as that the devil can never get an advantage over us. Oh, let us seek to enter into it! I tell you my own experience in this very thing is this: I distrust myself more than ever, I own before God more than ever my own weakness and helplessness, and I have continually cried to God to keep me from the craftiness and the deceit of the wicked one, for were I left to myself, aged as I am, and long as I have walked in the ways of God, and in some little degree also in the fear of God, to His honour and glory, in love and holiness-yet with all this, were I left to myself my life would end just as Asa's did. For thirty years he had glorified God greatly; but in the last two years of his life he dishonoured God deeply. So, on account of my own weakness, my prayer continually is, "Lord, grant that I may finish my course with joy, and not to the shame and dishonour of Thy Holy Name."

"For Thine is the kingdom, and the power, and the glory, forever. Amen." These words bring before us "the Why" to expect answers to our prayers. The Kingdom is the Lord's, He, therefore, is able to do it. He is the Mighty One, the Powerful One. "Thine is the Kingdom, and the power, and the glory, forever." Thou, O God, art not changing, there is no variation found in Thee. Thou art able to succour us. This is still further confirmed by the word "Amen." Yes! So it shall be. In this evil world we shall greatly cheer ourselves and comfort ourselves by this very statement here, "Thine is the Kingdom, and the power, and the glory, forever, Amen." Oh, how precious the prospect, that we do not speak into the air, but that we speak to the loving heart of God Almighty, Who can do everything and Who is willing on behalf of His children to do everything that is for their real blessing in Christ.

Now, in the next and last two verses, we have that which I have already referred to. "For if ye forgive men their trespasses, your Heavenly Father will also forgive you; but if ye forgive not men their trespasses, neither will your Father forgive your trespasses." Here we see that not only are we not warranted in expecting answers to our prayers if we do not forgive our fellow-men, when they have offended against us, and have done things which are improper; but also we shall lose the knowledge and the enjoyment which springs from the consciousness of the forgiveness of our own sins. It is plainly stated, "If ye forgive men their trespasses, your Heavenly Father will also forgive you, but if ye forgive not men their trespasses, neither will your Father forgive your trespasses." And I believe that in this we have the secret why in our day there are found so many true children of God whose life and deportment indicate that they are believers in Christ, but who yet do not enjoy the forgiveness of their sins. In the case of not a few we have reason to believe it originates from there being something in their mind which they seem to be unable to pass over regarding offences they have suffered from others, and that they have not forgiven. If this is the case they cannot wonder why they do not themselves enjoy the knowledge of the forgiveness of their own sins.

Now, this little portion on which we have been meditating says to us afresh, "What an unspeakably blessed thing it is to be a child of God." Thus I have found it during the past seventy-one years and five months that I have been a believer in the Lord Jesus! Oh, I cannot express to any who are not believers in the Lord Jesus Christ what they lost by staying away from Him! There are so many who suppose that to become a Christian is a wretched and miserable thing, that to become a believer in Christ and to give the heart to the Lord Jesus shuts us out from life, from everything, and from every particle of enjoyment. A false notion altogether. The very reverse, the very reverse is the case! I repeat what I have said more than once, that with all my might, as a young man under twenty, I sought happiness in the things of this world, and I had the opportunity of finding it if it could be found in this way at all. I was passionately fond of the theatre; I was fond of the ballroom; at the card table, at the billiard table, and in all kinds of worldly societies I was found, and at the head of them very frequently as a leader; but instead of finding real, true happiness it was nothing but disappointment that I met with continually. At last I thought, "Oh, if only I could travel a great deal, how happy that would make me!" God allowed me to taste this. I travelled forty-three days in succession, day by day, day by day. I saw the most beautiful scenery to be seen under heaven; but after six weeks I became so sick of travelling that I could pass the most beautiful scenery without even looking at it. Five weeks after I found Jesus, I found my Heavenly Friend, and the very first evening I was lying peacefully on my bed as a forgiven sinner, in peace with God. I blessed and praised Him for it. And without having to say to me, "Now it must be out with the theatre, it must be out with the card table, it must be out with the ballroom"-without anyone speaking to me a word, for I had not seen a single Christian to converse with, that was a settled matter.

I was regenerated now, born again, having obtained spiritual life after I had been twenty years and five weeks dead in trespasses and sins. Therefore, I say, without anyone saying a single word to me, it was a settled matter that my whole life must be changed and altered. And thus it was; and what has been the result? I became instantly a very happy young man, and I have been a happy man in middle-aged years, and I am a happy man, yes, an exceedingly happy man, greatly advanced as I am now in years. O,

>"If all the world my Jesus knew,
>All the world would love Him too."

But it is because the unconverted think it is a miserable thing to come to Christ that they stay away from Him. The truth is this: That only, only, only through faith in the Lord Jesus can real, true happiness be obtained. Therefore, any who have put this to themselves and stayed away from Christ, let them do so no longer, let them own that they are sinners, deserving nothing but punishment, and put their trust alone in Jesus for the salvation of their souls, and the result will be that they will obtain peace and joy in God, even as I found it when I was brought to Christ. May God grant that this may speak to the hearts of those who as yet have been going on thoughtlessly and carelessly and unconcerned about the things of Heaven.

Chapter 4: The Beloved of the Lamb.

A Sermon preached at Bethesda Chapel, Great George Street Bristol, on Whit-Sunday Evening, June 6th, 1897.

Revelation 7:9-17.

"AFTER THIS I beheld, and, lo, a great multitude, which no man could number, of all nations, and kindreds, and people and tongues, stood before the throne, and before the Lamb, clothed with white robes, and palms in their hands." At present, to all outward appearance, the number of the believers in the Lord Jesus Christ is small, in comparison with the vast number of those who do not believe in Him. But it will not always be thus; the day is coming when innumerable multitudes will be found to belong to Christ. O how precious to remember this! How deeply important to dwell on it, to seek more and more to apprehend it, to comfort ourselves by it, and to be stimulated through it to labour that we individually may be God's instruments of adding to this vast multitude! What an encouragement this for missionary labours! What an encouragement this to speak to souls about their salvation! What an encouragement, also, to seek to win the young, the middle-aged, and all classes of persons for the Lord, by Sunday schools, ragged schools, and in any way that will tend to it!

But in an especial manner it should lead us, individually to stand before God, and to offer ourselves for missionary service, if we have not done it yet. If the Lord accept us, He will use us for the praise of His Name; if the Lord does not accept us, we have done our part, in ourselves. Still further, if we do not go out individually to heathen countries, we may yet be instrumental in glorifying God in connection with missionary labours. We can help the missionaries with the means with which God will entrust us, and we can help them by our prayers, by writing to them a word of comfort, and a word of encouragement, and in a variety of ways besides we may be instrumental in helping missionary operations. A deeply important verse is this, full of comfort, full of encouragement, full of exhortation to do what we can that we may be instruments to increase this great multitude won for the Lord.

"I beheld, and lo, a great multitude, which no man could number." It is out of the power of any human being to count the vast number of the saved ones. "Which no man could number, of all nations, and kindreds, and people, and tongues stood before the throne." Notice the word "stood;"

that shows the attitude of a servant. All these elect holy angels stood before the throne; all these saved ones, this innumerable multitude of all nations and tribes and peoples and languages were in the attitude of servants before Jehovah. "Stood before the throne and before the Lamb." The Lamb, as you all know, whenever the expression is used, has reference to our Lord Jesus Christ, by reason of the atonement that He made. "They were clothed with white robes." White robes! This has reference to the power of the blood of the Lord Jesus Christ. Naturally, we stand before God in filthy garments, spiritually; and these filthy garments we cannot ourselves wash and make white, so that God can be satisfied with us. We cannot give righteousness to ourselves. We have none. All our own righteousness in Scripture is compared to filthy rags. Whether we see it or not; whether we readily allow it or not, this is the statement of God: our own goodness, merit, worthiness, and righteousness are as "filthy rags."

Now these filthy rags can never enter into heaven! God cannot bear spiritual filth in heaven! All of this character must be taken away: the spiritual filth must be removed, and the only way to remove it is by the power of the blood of the Lord Jesus Christ. Now, a great practical question, therefore, regarding everyone is this, "How is it with me?" We should ask ourselves, "How is it with my spiritual robes; are they white and clean?" "Am I brought into such a state as that God can receive me into heaven?" If I have not yet seen that I am a sinner; if I have not yet confessed before God that I am a sinner; if I have not yet put my trust solely in the merits of the Lord Jesus Christ, and in His atoning blood, then I am not prepared for heaven! But I am come to this. This is not a salvation for a few chosen ones, or a few hundreds, nor even a salvation of a few thousands; but of an innumerable multitude saved by the power of the blood of the Lord Jesus Christ. And as they were saved, and deserved nothing but punishment, so I (we should say to ourselves individually), even I, may be saved, if I seek salvation in God's appointed way-seeking not to obtain it by my own goodness, merit, and worthiness, but through Jesus Christ. This innumerable company, every one of them obtained salvation through Jesus Christ, and thus may I obtain it. But in no other way.

Many persons say to themselves, "Well, it is true that it has not yet been all right with me, as it might have been and as it ought to have been; but I have tried now to turn over another leaf; I would seek now to live differently from what I have been doing, and thus I shall make up for past shortcomings, and failures, and sins." This is a soul-destroying error! We never, never, never can make up for one single sin of which we have been guilty, for if we failed in one particular only, if it were possible that we should be in such a state that we had fallen short but by one sin, that would be enough for our perdition, for we should then have broken the whole law; and as long as we trusted in ourselves for salvation, this broken law would bring destruction upon us. Therefore, we must look away from ourselves to Christ, and Him alone. God sent Him into the world in order that He not only might fulfil all the commandments which we have broken times without number, and thus work out a righteousness in which we can be accepted by God, but He also bore the punishment in our room and stead for our disobedience. We must, therefore, hide ourselves in Christ; that is, look away entirely from our own goodness, merit, and worthiness - of which we have none, none, none-and put our entire trust in the Lord Jesus.

Then, let us remember we must have "white robes," else we cannot enter into the presence of God. Our own sins, which are compared to filthy garments, must be removed, and we must solely and simply trust in the merits and sufferings of the Lord Jesus Christ, and thus, by the power of His atonement, be made clean from all our sins. O how precious! Now this is my comfort, having been guilty of numberless transgressions as a young man, having also failed and come short in a variety of ways since my conversion, though not living in gross sin: yet failing in action, in word, in thought, though hating sin and loving holiness-this is my comfort, I am standing before God in white robes, clean, and spotless, as if I had never in my whole life been guilty of one single sin. And into this state I have been brought through faith in the Lord Jesus; and into this state not merely I have been brought, but all who believe in Jesus, who trust in Him alone for salvation! O how comforting is this! The dread of God, the fear of death, the fear of eternity stops completely when entering into the work of the Lord Jesus, and appropriating it to ourselves! Now see to it, beloved Christian friends, that you individually do, if you have not yet done so, derive all the comfort which God intends us to derive from this expression, "White robes."

"And palms in their hands." The palm was in ancient times the sign of victory. And this innumerable multitude, every one of them having a palm in his or her hand, declares that victory has been obtained. Victory through the blood of the Lamb. Victory through the power of Jesus Christ, Who gave it to them. Victory obtained for us individually, because He loves us with an eternal, unchangeable love, "He Who has begun a good work in us will carry it on by the power of His Spirit," and so at the last receive us to glory. O how precious this is! At present we are in spiritual conflict. Satan is not conquered yet. Satan still is our great enemy and fights against us, and often and often obtains, in some way or another, an advantage over us--if it be not in the way of leading us to an open fall, there are some words escaping us which ought not to; there are some thoughts found in us which ought not to be; and even, now and then, an action which is not altogether according to the Christ-like state in which we ought to be found. But all this will come to an end. The blessed Jesus, Who has begun a good work in us, will finish it, and we shall have individually (weak and feeble and worthless though we are in ourselves), the victory, through Jesus Christ.

Now this innumerable multitude "Cried with a loud voice, saying, ' Salvation to our God, which sitteth upon the throne, and unto the Lamb.'" Notice this particularly! They ascribe salvation to God and to the Lamb; to the Father and to the Son; to Jehovah and to our Lord Jesus Christ. They do not say, "I was very prayerful; I was very conscientious; I never gave way to anything contrary to the mind of God." Nothing of the kind! The very reverse! Salvation is ascribed by everyone of the saved ones to God the Father, and to God the Son, the Lord Jesus, Who is found here under the figure of the Lamb. "They cried with a loud voice." It is especially also to be noticed that they did not merely whisper it now and then, a few times; but with a loud voice they declared it, that people might hear it, because it was the joy of their hearts to ascribe salvation to God, and to the Lord Jesus Christ, and take not the least credit to themselves. This will be the case with every one of the saved ones. Fellow-believers, we shall all, from our inmost souls, ascribe entirely our salvation to God and to the Lord Jesus, and that we did nothing whatever, but simply, like beggars, accepted what was given to us!

"And all the angels stood round about the throne, and about the elders, and the four beasts"-that means the four living creatures, in contradistinction to the four great worldly powers that will brood over Gentile sinners-"and fell before the throne on their faces, and worshipped God." Notice this again, the holy, unfallen angels stood round about the throne;" stood, indicating the position of servants before the Master "stood round about the throne and about the elders," representing the Church, and the four living creatures, and fell before the throne on their faces," in deep humility of soul, ascribing salvation to God the Father and to the Lord Jesus, "and worshipped God," praising and adoring Him for what He had done for them, "Saying, Amen"-that is, "Even so is it. "Blessing"--that is, praise in the highest degree-"and glory, and wisdom, and thanksgiving, and honour, and power, and might, be unto our God for ever and ever, Amen." This expresses the deep gratitude felt on the part of the redeemed ones; and thus it will be with us. If there is a little praise and a little thanksgiving now found in our hearts, in the highest degree we shall adore, and praise, and magnify, and worship the Lord for what He has done for us in Christ Jesus. And then again, to this they set their "Amen," that is, ascribing all from their heart to God.

"And one of the elders answered, saying unto me, 'What are these which are arrayed in white robes, and whence came they?' And I said unto him, 'Sir, thou knowest!'" The question was asked the apostle John as to whence these individuals came; and he confesses his ignorance. "Sir, thou knowest"-that means, in other words, "I do not know, but thou dost know it, and thou art able to tell me;" and through this confession of his ignorance he obtains the information. And this is just what we have to do before God, not to make our boast that we know everything, that we are already instructed to the very highest degree, that we cannot be instructed; but, on the contrary, to own again and again, when we read the Scriptures and find something that we do not understand, that we are ignorant of the meaning of the passage, and ask God that He would graciously be pleased to teach us. We shall find that He is ready to do it. And this instance of how even an apostle confessed his ignorance should be a particular encouragement to us to be ready on our part also to confess our ignorance; for we know that he was not only greatly honoured, but he was a believer who had been for a long time in service, in great service, who for a very long time had been an Apostle, and who was now at the close of his earthly pilgrimage, for he was about ninety years of age, but he was not ashamed to confess his ignorance. And so we should never be ashamed before God to confess our ignorance, for that is the very way to increase our knowledge. If we humble ourselves before God, He will further and further instruct us.

"'Sir, thou knowest.' And he said unto me, 'These are they which came out of great tribulation'"-more exactly, "'which came out of the great tribulation,'" having especial reference to what they had had to pass through, and bringing before us also that through which we may have yet to pass-"and have washed their robes, and made them white in the blood of the Lamb." Here we have on no account to suppose that the great tribulation had made their robes white, but the blood of the Lamb; and we must never lose sight of the fact that no trials, no afflictions, make us white. They may be helpful to us, they may do us good spiritually, they ought to do us good spiritually; for on this very account, trials, sufferings, pains, sickness, afflictions, are sent to us, to be a blessing to us-but they never can make our robes white. The blood of Jesus Christ alone can accomplish this. "And have washed their robes, and made them white in the blood of the Lamb; therefore are they before the throne." Not on account of the great tribulation are they there, but because their robes were made white by the blood of the Lamb; that is, by the atoning work of the Lord Jesus Christ. "Therefore are they before the throne of God."

Now comes something else. "And serve Him day and night in His temple." "Serve Him day and night." Some persons have an idea that heaven consists in singing away our time, so that one hundred years after the other we shall be singing, and that the joys of heaven consist in doing nothing. This is a great mistake. If we work and serve the Lord a little, it is held out as a great honour, a great privilege of serving the Lord in eternity. There is one verse, particularly, pointing out this in the last chapter of the Book of Revelation, the third verse, where it is stated, "There shall be no more curse, but the throne of God and of the Lamb shall be in it, and His servants shall serve Him." Notice, this is held out as the greatest honour, privilege, enjoyment, and blessing-that the servants of the Living God shall serve Him; that is, have the great honour, the great privilege, bestowed upon them of serving the Lord, and just in the degree in which they have now the mind of Christ, in which they look at being allowed to serve the Lord as an honour, as a privilege, and not as a burden, not as an irksome task.

I myself, have now for many a long year, again and again and again, asked the Lord that He would yet allow me to have the great honour, the great privilege, the great enjoyment to serve Him, to labour for Him. So far from considering it a burden, an irksome task, the very reverse of this; and just in the degree in which we are happy in the Lord, so we shall look upon serving Him as a great privilege, as a particular honour, a particular enjoyment bestowed upon us.

"And they shall see His Face, and His Name shall be in their foreheads." Now, that we find in the last chapter. Here is a reference also in the 15th verse of the 7th chapter, "Therefore"-because they have washed their robes and made them white in the blood of the Lamb- "therefore are they before the throne of God, and serve Him day and night."

And when you and I, as believers, shall be found at the last in this place, and in this state, and actually do serve the Lord night and day, and we shall adore and praise Him for bestowing this honour upon us to do any little thing for Him. "And He that sitteth on the throne shall dwell among them." God completely near, in our midst; we shall look at Him without the least particle of dread or fear, because the guilt is completely gone from the conscience, through the power of the atoning blood of the Lord Jesus Christ. O the blessedness of all this; and these are not merely simple phrases, but these statements are brought before us as realities, which hereafter will be found true in our own happy experience.

Then in the last two verses we have before us the exceedingly blessed state in which we shall be found, when the curse has been completely removed. "They shall hunger no more, neither thirst anymore." That is not literally hunger, nor literally thirst; but spiritually no longer hungering nor thirsting, having obtained to the full everything which even the renewed heart can desire. O think of the blessedness, the wondrous blessedness of all this! And yet with all these statements in Holy Writ, it is again and again found that when persons are converted, they are pitied as being very silly and foolish persons, because it is thought they have to be wretched, as if it were a miserable thing to be regenerated, to be born again. Why, the truth is there is no real happiness, and can be none, till we are brought to know Jesus, and all of us who are believers in Christ know it from our own experience. We sought happiness in the beggarly pleasures of the world, and we sometimes even thought we had obtained it; but a little while longer and we found we had been deceiving ourselves-that no real, true happiness could be found anywhere else but in the Lord Jesus. And we know, from experience, that what we did obtain was through faith in Christ.

"They shall hunger no more, neither thirst anymore; neither shall the sun light on them, nor any heat"-that is, the sun shall not strike them in a painful way, in an unpleasant way, as in tropical countries. While I was once on my missionary tours, going through India, I had again and again to hear from beloved missionary brethren what a trial to them was the excessive heat, this being struck by the sun. And at last, I myself knew this, from my own experience, for after I had laboured for forty weeks in Calcutta, with the heat at 110 degrees, it came to this, that I could only lie on my couch, without being able to do anything at all; and when I sought medical advice regarding it, the physician told me, "At the risk of your life you stay one day longer here; you must at once go to the hills." And only when I was in an atmosphere of three or four thousand feet above the sea, life returned again, as it were, and I got into a different state. All this explains what is meant here, "neither shall the sun light on them," that is, strike on them, "nor any heat." The curse being gone, this, too, will completely go, and so in our glorified bodies we shall not have the least inconvenience regarding any of these things.

"For the Lamb which is in the midst of the throne shall feed them, and shall lead them unto living fountains of waters, and God shall wipe away all tears from their eyes." Completely near God! Completely near the Lord Jesus, in His happy presence habitually, day after day, year after year, one hundred years after the other, one thousand years after the other, one million years after the other; and unspeakably happy continually, everything that would try us removed completely, because the curse is gone. "God shall wipe away all tears from their eyes." This is the blessed privilege not merely of one, or of the other, such as Paul, or Peter, or James, or John, but the great privilege of the weakest, feeblest child of God now on earth. O how blessed! How unspeakably blessed is the lot of everyone who is a disciple of Jesus! Therefore, instead of allowing these persons to pity us, because we are awake spiritually, and made to come to Christ, we have rather to tell them how exceedingly happy we are, through believing in Jesus. Now are there any present who are not yet believers in the Lord? You may be looking forward to especial enjoyment at Whitsuntide, and be saying to yourselves, "O when Whitsuntide comes, how happy I shall be." That was just the case with me when I was a boy. Whitsuntide was particularly a pleasant time, and in the little town where I was brought up there was much going on at that time. But Whitsuntide lasted only a few days! At last, however, when I was twenty years of age, I found Jesus, of Whom I had never heard as an unconverted young man, for though I had thirty tutors in the high classical school in which I was for nine years to be prepared for the University, it being the wish of my father that I should become a clergyman, yet not one of them ever spoke to me about my soul. One day, when in deep trial, infidel books were put into my hand, which I shuddered to look at and returned, but never did anyone speak to me about Jesus until I was just past twenty. Then being led into a little religious meeting, through the advice of a friend, I found Jesus. I entered this meeting as completely dead in sin as any young man could be. I left the house as a happy young disciple of the Lord Jesus, and have been a happy man ever since, now seventy-one years and seven months. Therefore, instead of our being to be pitied when brought to Jesus, if people understood what is meant by coming to Him, and trusting in Him they, themselves would be in earnest to care about their souls. But because they are ignorant as to what it means to believe on Christ, so they look on us with pity and compassion.

It is an unspeakably blessed thing, even for this life, to be a believer in Christ; but what will it be when at last we actually enter upon the glory, and become perfect in His likeness, perfectly free from sin, in every way ready, moment by moment, to glorify God, so that His Will will only have to be presented to us, and instantly we shall be ready to carry it out! That day is coming, be sure of it. It will come, and therefore should there be any present who have not as yet surrendered their heart to the Lord, O, my dear young friends, O, my dear fellow-sinners of middle age, O, my fellow-sinners greatly advanced in life, if you have not yet given your heart to the Lord, hasten to do It without a moment's longer delay.

Be in earnest! Own before God that you are a sinner, that you deserve nothing but punishment, and ask Him in pity and compassion to look upon you, and to help you to put your trust in Jesus. Thus the blessing will come, as assuredly as you really desire to obtain it. God grant that it may be so, for Jesus' sake. Amen.

Chapter 5: Naaman and Gehazi.

A Sermon preached at Bethesda Chapel, Great George Street, Bristol, on Sunday Evening, May 2nd, 1897·

2 Kings 5.

A GREAT MAN was Naaman, a very great man, and not only so, but a very rich man, as we shall presently see by the illustration we have here. "But he was a leper." O, how frequently does the Lord act in this way, that with all the glory and honour in connection with great standing in the world, amid the admiration of the world; there is some trial, some affliction, some special trial, or some special affliction associated. Thus it was here. This man was the chief captain of the mighty host of the King of Syria. God had greatly blessed him in that position, for through his instrumentality victory, great victory, had been gained. Personally, also he was "a mighty man in valour." "But he was a leper."

Now, naturally, the desire under such circumstances was that there might be found a remedy for the disease; but it was not to be had. Yea, notwithstanding all that medical skill has been able to accomplish in these hundreds of years, and thousands of years, there never yet has been found a remedy for leprosy. It has been sought after, continually sought after, but without avail. Now, as I stated, Naaman would say, "O, I wish I could get rid of this leprosy;" and at last he did get rid of it. But this very leprosy was the means of his conversion; he would never have got into contact with the prophet in Samaria had it not been for the leprosy. And thus God in our own case, again and again, allows a trial, a great trial, a very heavy trial, in order to bestow on us great blessing. But for the leprosy, speaking after the manner of men, the salvation of his soul never would have come! God, however, overruled all this to the blessing of his soul, and thus God overrules again and again in our own case, so that the greatest trials turn out the greatest blessings.

Here I set my own case, and refer to my own experience, in a long Christian life. I have never passed through a single trial (and I have had hundreds of them), but invariably it has turned out a blessing to me; and I have found that my greatest trials and my greatest difficulties have become my greatest blessings in the end! I mention this particularly for the comfort and encouragement of young believers: to let God work as He wills. A little maid, a young girl, is here used by the Lord to bring about a great work. God is a wonder-working God! He has ten times ten thousand different ways of working, but He always does His work and always manages things to turn out to the glory of His Name!

Who would have thought that this poor little maid, who was taken captive by the Syrians, would be the instrument in bringing about the restoration of the chief captain of the host of Syria, and, more than this, to bring about the salvation of his soul? The prophet could not do it of himself; but the prophet was to be a further instrument in bringing about the restoration, by the power of God Almighty! "And she (the maid) said unto her mistress, 'Would God my lord were with the prophet that is in Samaria, for he would recover him of his leprosy'". Now this might have been said, and no notice taken of it, or, if there had been one willing to take notice, yet he might not have been in the right quarter to hear; but to bring about real blessing, we read, "One went in, and told his lord." That is, her master, the chief captain of the host, was informed. "Thus and thus said the maid that is of the land of Israel. And the King of Syria said, 'Go to, go, and I will send a letter unto the King of Israel;' and he departed, and took with him ten talents of silver, and six thousand pieces of gold, and ten changes of raiment."

He considered that as the blessing sought after was so great, he must take an immense present to give to the prophet. It was a matter of such exceeding great importance to be restored to health, to have the leprosy removed. Now here we see, what I stated before, that Naaman was not only a great leader, a great soldier, a mighty captain, and personally of great valour, but he was, in addition to this, an exceedingly rich man. In the first place, as a fee for restoration, he took ten talents of silver. That means, of our money, £3,422, for the Jewish talent was equal to £ 342 3s. 9d. Then he was not merely content with ten talents of silver, but took also six thousand pieces of gold. In the Hebrew what is called here a piece of gold represents considerably more than a pound sterling; therefore, these six thousand pieces of gold made about £10,000 more. In all about £ 13,422 was the amount he took as a fee to the prophet for recovering him from his leprosy. This shows how immensely rich he was! Ten changes of raiment also, of the value no doubt of not a few pounds, were included in the gift.

"And he brought the letter to the King of Israel, saying, 'Now when this letter is come unto thee, behold, I have therewith sent Naaman, my servant, to thee, that thou mayest recover him of his leprosy.' And it came to pass, when the King of Israel had read the letter, that he rent his clothes and said, 'Am I God, to kill and to make alive, that this man doth send unto me to recover a man of his leprosy? Wherefore consider, I pray you, and see how he seeketh a quarrel against me.'" The King of Syria, of course, understanding nothing of the miraculous manner in which the prophet might restore the leper of his leprosy, thought it was simply a matter of power that was to be exercised, and all he had to do was to give a letter of commendation to his chief captain Naaman, and that then the matter would be settled by the King of Israel. But when the King of Israel read the letter he was altogether astonished to receive such a communication, and considered that as it was quite out of his power to do the thing asked, the letter had been written to seek an occasion against him to begin a war.

"And it was so, when Elisha the man of God had heard that the King of Israel had rent his clothes, that he sent to the King, saying, 'Wherefore hast thou rent thy clothes? Let him come now to me, and he shall know that there is a prophet in Israel.'" It was to Elisha that the little Jewish maid had referred. "So Naaman came with his horses, and with his chariot, and stood at the door of the house of Elisha." He did not go in. It was beyond him, in his pride and high-mindedness, such a great man as he was. He remained quiet in his chariot, and expected that the prophet would come out to him and cure him there. "And Elisha sent a messenger unto him, saying, 'Go and wash in the Jordan seven times, and thy flesh shall come again to thee, and thou shalt be clean.' But Naaman was wroth, and went away, and said, 'Behold, I thought, he will surely come out to me, and stand and call on the Name of the Lord his God, and strike his hand over the place and recover the leper. Are not Abana and Pharpar, rivers of Damascus, better than all the waters of Israel? May I not wash in them, and be clean? So he turned and went away in a rage.'"

This passage is exceedingly instructive to everyone of us. "I thought he would do so and so." He laid down a rule how the prophet should act. And thus are we continually in danger, when we read statements in the Word of God which do not agree with our preconceived notions, saying, "How can this be?" "How is this possible?" "I think so and so about it." "I think it ought to have been thus stated." Just acting like this Naaman, when he said, "Behold, I thought, he will surely come out to me, and stand and call on the Name of the Lord his God, and strike his hand over the place" (move his hand up and down over the place, that is the idea), "and recover the leper." O, let us ask God to keep us from such a spirit as Naaman manifested in this case.

But then he goes further, "Are not Abana and Pharpar rivers of Damascus, better than all the waters of Israel? May I not wash in them, and be clean? So he turned and went away in a rage." Now, in the next verse, we see how much wiser his servants were than their master. "And his servants came near, and spake unto him, and said, 'My father.'" He was not literally their father, but this was an honourable way of addressing him. "' My father, if the prophet had bid thee do some great thing, wouldest thou not have done it?'" If, for instance, he had said, "Run a thousand miles time after time," he would not have considered it anything too much. Or if he had said, "Beat thyself a thousand times for five minutes each time, very severely," he would not have considered it too great a thing. But because it was such a very little thing, he despised it. Here we find the wisdom of the servant above the wisdom of the master. "How much rather then, when he saith to thee, 'Wash and be clean?'" Such a very little thing.

Well, this speech of the servants had an effect on him. "Then went he down and dipped himself seven times in Jordan, according to the saying of the man of God; and his flesh came again like unto the flesh of a little child, and he was clean." Now, it is a very remarkable thing that in the oldest translation of the Old Testament, called as many of you know already, the Septuagint, which is written in Greek, the passage is, "Be baptized himself seven times in Jordan," bringing before us the meaning of baptizing. "And his flesh came again like unto the flesh of a little child, and he was clean."

Now, see, how the man instantaneously is completely altered. "And he returned to the man of God, he and all his company, and came and stood before him." Not now remaining seated in his chariot, in his pride and high-mindedness, as the chief captain of the host of the King of Syria; but, as a humble servant, standing before the prophet. "And he said, 'Behold, now I know that there is no God, in all the earth, but in Israel; now, therefore, I pray thee, take a blessing of thy servant.'" He had now come to the knowledge of the true and living God. He had been an idolator before, nothing but an idolator, and an idolator all his life. But now, through the instrumentality of the miracle which had been wrought on him, in restoring him of his leprosy, curing him completely, he is an altered man altogether.

"Take a blessing of thy servant." That means, "Now, take all this silver and gold which I have brought to thee, and these ten changes of raiment; take all this." That is what he meant when he said, "I pray thee, take a blessing of thy servant," for he had brought this enormous sum of money as a reward for curing him of his leprosy. Now, see how the prophet acts. But he said, " As the Lord liveth before Whom I stand'" ("As Jehovah liveth, Whose servant I am," that is the meaning of the words, "Before Whom I stand "), "I will receive none." This prophet sought the glory of God. If he had taken the vast sum of money offered, it would have been considered that he wrought miracles for the purpose of obtaining money. But that was altogether far from this holy man's purpose. All was done to the glory of God. "And he urged him to take it; but he refused." He would not take one small silver coin as a recompense. Not one single change of raiment. He took nothing whatever! The glory of God was dearer to his heart than all the immense sum of gold and silver which Naaman brought to give him.

"And Naaman said, 'Shall there not then, I pray thee, be given to thy servant two mules' burden of earth? For thy servant will thenceforth offer neither burnt offering nor sacrifice unto other gods, but unto the Lord.'" See how complete the change was! Without a word being said by the prophet to him, he had obtained from God enough light at once to see that he could not remain any longer an idolator. As to his worship, there must be a complete alteration in his whole life. He saw that the worship in which he had been engaged up to that time was altogether contrary to the mind of God, that it was idolatry, and hateful to Him; that he had been worshipping devils, instead of the true and living God.

He desired instantaneously to become altogether different; and without a single word having been spoken to him on the subject, he considered that now he had to alter all this. He must bring his offering to God, and he conceived that there was no better altar to be obtained than one made of the earth of the country of Israel. For this reason, he desired "two mules' burden of earth." See in what a brief time God can work real, true conversion in the hearts of persons! And to make this practical we are to look upon our unconverted parents, or unconverted children, or unconverted wives or husbands, however far from God they may be now, and remember how it is in the power of God very, very quickly, in a brief moment, to change their hearts completely. Such a portion as this tells us how readily God can alter things. There is Paul's conversion before us. The voice from heaven, "Saul, Saul, why persecutest thou Me?" instantly brought about a complete change in the heart of this persecutor of the disciples of the Lord Jesus Christ.

And there is Manasseh's case; a most fearfully wicked one. We have not an instance, in Holy Scripture, of one more abominable and more wicked than this Manasseh was. But the Almighty imposed a terrible judgment on him, with the result that he was brought to the knowledge of the true living God, and became an entirely altered person. This abominable wretch, this most awful sinner of sinners! See what God can do. The man is completely altered. He who had made Jerusalem almost to swim in blood, on account of the numberless innocent persons whom he had murdered. An exceeding encouragement this is, and it brings before us the exhortation under no circumstances to give up prayer, but continually to look at the power of God, in His love, to listen to our supplications.

"And Naaman said, 'Shall there not then, I pray thee, be given to thy servant two mules' burden of earth. In this thing the Lord pardon thy servant, that when my master goeth unto the house of Rimmon to worship there, and he leaneth on my hand, and I bow myself in the house of Rimmon, when I bow down myself in the house of Rimmon, the Lord pardon thy servant in this thing.'" A remark that which shows us the enlightenment given to Naaman. He reasoned, "I am going back to Damascus, and when there, I, as the chief captain of the host of the King of Syria, shall have to accompany my master when he worships in the house of the idol Rimmon. My master will expect that when he bows before Rimmon, I bow too; and what will become of me if I bow not down, as my master the king does?" Therefore, he brings this before the prophet.

Now, naturally, one might have expected that the prophet would say, "O, Naaman, this would be very wicked of you; thou must rather give up thy position as chief captain than bow down before this idol. Thou wilt dishonour God, the true and living God, in doing so!" But what does the prophet say? "And he said unto him, 'Go in peace.'" That means, before Naaman could get to his master's, the Lord would enlighten him more and more; for he had shown already how in these few hours after his conversion, he had obtained such an exceeding great amount of knowledge that he could no longer carryon his idol worship as before, and, therefore, wanted another altar altogether, and would on this account take some of the earth away out of the land of Israel, in order to carry on a completely different worship from what he had been engaged in before. Therefore, the prophet considered, "Let him alone; the Holy Spirit will instruct him further and further, for he has given proof already how greatly He has advanced him since he dipped himself and washed himself in Jordan."

It was on this account that the prophet said, "Go in peace." Not that he would countenance idolatry, but that at present he was too weak to be fully enlightened about everything. Just such a case as we find in the Gospels. The Lord Jesus Christ had many things more to say to his disciples, but they could not bear them; and, therefore, He did not speak, further and further to them. For this very reason, the prophet said nothing; but left it to the power of the Spirit of God, not merely to enlighten, but to strengthen him, for what he had to do. And we have the fullest reason to believe that Naaman, on whom the king had leaned in going to the house of Rimmon, no longer proceeded as he had before.

But Gehazi, the servant of Elisha, the man of God, said, 'Behold, my master has spared Naaman this Syrian, in not receiving at his hands that which he brought; but as the Lord liveth, I will run after him and take somewhat of him.' So Gehazi followed after Naaman; and when Naaman saw him running after him, he lighted down from the chariot to meet him, and said, 'Is all well?'; and he said, 'All is well; my master hath sent me, saying, "Behold, even now, there be come to me from Mount Ephraim two young men of the sons of the prophets; give them, I pray thee, a talent of silver, and two changes of garments." A complete falsehood, a fabrication of the whole, in order that he might get money for himself. And he did get the money for himself; but the lies he had uttered brought a most horrible judgment.

" And Naaman said, 'Be content; take two talents;' and he urged him, and bound two talents of silver in two bags, with two changes of garments, and laid them upon two of his servants; and they bare them before him." Naaman was ready at once to do what he was asked by giving two talents-which, of our money, is £684, 8s.-besides two changes of garments; and it was a heavy load for two servants to carry. "And they bare them before him. And when he came to the tower"-rather to the elevation of the hill, Samaria being built on a hill, which he had come down in order to get to Naaman- "he took them from their hand, and bestowed them in the house; and he let the men go, and they departed." Having got the money, he put it away in some secret place in the house to hide it. "But he went in, and stood before his master. And Elisha said unto him, 'Whence cometh thou, Gehazi?' And he said, 'Thy servant went no whither.'" Ready to utter lie after lie. "And he said unto him, 'Went not mine heart with thee, when the man turned again from his chariot to meet thee? Is it a time to receive money, and to receive garments, and oliveyards, and vineyards, and sheep, and oxen, and menservants, and maidservants?' "

"O, Gehazi, thou hast not cared in the least about the honour of Jehovah!" We imagine the prophet saying, "I refused what was offered to me, and would take nothing whatever, in order that God might be glorified by my declining to accept a recompense for restoring him of his leprosy; and thou hast uttered lies, thou hast taken this money contrary to the mind of God. This is no time to receive money under such circumstances; it is no time to receive a profit, to receive garments, and oliveyards, and vineyards, and sheep, and oxen, and menservants, and maidservants, as thou art looking after, and craving to obtain, by the money which thou, through lies, hast now obtained."

"The leprosy, therefore, of Naaman, shall cleave unto thee, and unto thy seed for ever. And he went out from his presence a leper as white as snow." The ordinary way in which God acts is that He does not, under like ,circumstances, bestow such terrible affliction, in the way of chastisement, on those who have been guilty as this Gehazi was; but this judgment is to bring before us how painful sin is to God, and how in the end He will visit wickedness upon those who offend Him. And this particularly reminds us of the fact, since all of us more or less are sinners, though we may not have been guilty of such sins as Gehazi was, that we need the atonement of the Lord Jesus Christ, in order to make us clean from our sins.

Therefore, the solemn question occurs in reference to everyone of us, "Have we obtained this atonement for ourselves? Have we individually been really and truly cleansed from our sins, through faith in the Lord Jesus, so that the blood of Christ becomes our atonement, to make us clean from all our numberless transgressions?" How do we stand before God regarding our sins? O, what will become of us if for one single sin of which we have been guilty, we have to suffer! For every one of our numberless transgressions we need the blood of Christ to make us clean; and if we are standing before God on the ground of our own goodness, merits, and worthiness, it would be certain to be our ruin forever. E very one of us, the very best among us, needs a Saviour. And trusting in Him, depending on

Him, the greatest sinner need not despair, for there is power in the blood of Christ to make all clean from their sins.

Now, then, let us remember how in Naaman's case, an exceeding great trial led to an exceeding great blessing, even the salvation of his soul. And though we may be saved already by having come to Christ, and therefore, though in this sense the blessing may not be so great as in the case of Naaman, this is certain: that God intends by every trial with which He visits us to bring a blessing in the end. Thus invariably I have found it.

Then let us remember how much a little maid may accomplish; how even a little maid may witness for God, and be His instrument in bringing about great blessing. Then let us further remember, in regard to the Holy Scriptures, that we have never to reason as Naaman did, "I thought," "I thought." It is not what we think, but what God thinks. God declares the truth, and our business is to accept it as He declares it. We have not to say, "O, I thought He would do so and so!" Let us not reason about the Word of God as if we knew better than God. He knows; and we have to learn. God is infinitely wise, and we are extremely ignorant. We have, therefore, to submit to what He says at all times, and under all circumstances.

Then, lastly, let the example of Gehazi be a warning to us. Though God does not in every case visit sin as He did here in the case of Gehazi; at the last He will have the account settled regarding our sins, and woe, woe, woe, unto us, if we are found standing on the ground of our own merit and worthiness, instead of hiding ourselves in Christ. The work must be His. Depending entirely upon His atoning work, knowing nothing in the matter of salvation but Christ, and from first to last, all, all, will be well throughout eternity.

Chapter 6: Underneath are the Everlasting Arms.

A Sermon preached at Bethesda Chapel, Great George Street, Bristol, on Sunday Evening, July 25th, 1897·

Deuteronomy 33:26-29.

THERE IS NONE like unto the God of Jeshurun, who rideth upon the heaven in thy help, and in His excellency on the sky." "Jeshurun" is the name for the Israelites; it means "the righteous ones." They are accounted thus on the ground of the work of the Messiah. In themselves most ungodly, very ungodly, often and often open idolators, and yet by reason of their union to the Messiah, they are called, "The righteous nation." In the first part of the chapter we have the blessing of each of the tribes. "Thy Thummim and thy Urim" (verse 8). Through their instrumentality, which was fixed in connection with their movements from the very first, the Israelites knew which way Jehovah would have them to go, how to act, and what to do under particular circumstances, when they desired to know the mind of God. "Let thy Thummim and thy Urim be with thy holy one."

After each of the twelve tribes of Israel had been individually blessed through the instrumentality of Moses, for the whole of Israel, the whole of Jeshurun (commencing with the 26th verse), there is a blessing pronounced. "There is none like unto the God of Jeshurun." This is what our hearts continually say regarding the Father of our Lord Jesus Christ, the only true and living God. "There is none like unto Thee;" and this should fill our hearts with great comfort, that we have to do with one, Who is alone by Himself, with Whom no one can be compared, Who is almighty as to power, Who is infinite as to love; wisdom, grace, mercy, long-suffering, forebearance, and in Whom every blessing is to be found. None like Him! "None like unto the God of Jeshurun!" Then, of Him it is said as to His power, "Who rideth upon the heaven," and He does it "in thy help." One Who rideth upon the heavens as almighty. It is only He can do it, and He does do it for our help. How precious! We are, therefore, beyond the power of our enemies, for on our side is He Who is able to ride on the clouds for our help! Who can do everything for our benefit-for that is the meaning of it. "Who rideth upon the heaven in thy help," or for the sake of helping thee; "for thy help."

"And in His excellency on the sky." In His almighty power, in His majesty, He rides on the sky. If this were continually before us, how peacefully we should pass on, remembering that our friend and helper in heaven can do everything, and not only can do everything, but is willing to do everything, for sinners who put their trust in the Lord Jesus Christ for salvation! The great business of life, therefore, in the first place, is to be reconciled to God by faith in the Lord Jesus Christ; and, in order that this may be the case, we have to own that we are sinners, that we deserve nothing but punishment, and then put our sole trust for salvation in the Lord Jesus Christ. The moment we do so, we are regenerated, we obtain spiritual life, we become the children of God, and as such the heirs of God, and joint-heirs with the Lord Jesus Christ; and this blessing we receive for eternity -it will never be taken from us, as assuredly as we put our trust in Jesus for salvation.

"The Eternal God is thy Refuge, and underneath are the Everlasting Arms; and He shall thrust out the enemy from before thee, and shall say, 'Destroy them!' " How precious again! "The Eternal God is thy Refuge," or thy dwelling-place. We are in Him, one with Him, shall not be separated from Him, because we dwell in Him; He is our dwelling-place. Just like what we read in the 90th Psalm. The Eternal God is our Refuge, our dwelling-place is found in Him, and underneath are the everlasting arms to protect us, to shield us, to keep us from harm, of every kind-for, in reality, we are kept from harm of every kind.

Sometimes it appears as if we had been injured, physically, mentally, spiritually; but it is often only in appearance, and nothing but in appearance. In reality we are watched over, cared for, looked after, and shielded and protected by the almighty power, and the eternal, unchangeable love of God, by which He has loved us in Christ Jesus. O, how precious! How precious this! And just in the degree in which we are enabled to realise it, to enter into it, and to appropriate it to ourselves, the result is peace and joy in the Holy Ghost. There is no trembling then, no fear then, no anxiety then, because we can say to ourselves, "God is on our side, God is for us; who can do us any harm?" Weak though we are, His everlasting arms are under us, to shield us, to watch over us!

"And he shall thrust out the enemy from before thee, and shall say, 'Destroy them.'" We have here especially to notice that before the Israelites ever got into the promised land, this was stated regarding them, and thus it came to pass. It was not their sword that obtained the land for them finally; but it was because God was on their side. "He thrust out the enemy from before them," and in a variety of ways this was done. Among all the ways, all the means used, was that God sent hornets against their enemies to drive them out and to destroy them. "He shall thrust out the enemy from before thee." And so it came to pass that they obtained the land, though they had to fight against seven great and mighty nations; but these seven nations could not stand before them, because God was against the enemies of the Israelites. God was for them, fighting habitually their battles, and appearing on their behalf at all times and under all circumstances. When there was a battle, great hailstones of the weight of more than one hundred pounds were smitten down on their enemies, whereby they were destroyed, so that more by the power of Jehovah, in one way or another manifested for the benefit of the Israelites, than by the sword of their own hand, were the enemies destroyed. "He shall thrust out the enemy from before thee." So He did, and so He destroyed them; because He spake the word, therefore it came to pass.

"Israel then shall dwell in safety alone." The enemies destroyed, the Israelites were left, and they occupied the land; but notice particularly this word, "Shall dwell in safety alone," because the real, true safety of the Israelites consisted in that they were separated from the Canaanitish nations. The moment they mixed up with the Canaanitish nations, their safety was at an end. And this is particularly to be noticed-that real, true spiritual blessing consists in separation from the ungodly. If we would really be in safety, we have to live in separation from this present evil world, and not needlessly mix up with the ungodly. In all temporal affairs, it may be necessary now and then that we meet with them and mix with them; but in all spiritual matters we should seek to walk in separation from the ungodly. In this, and in this alone, consists our real, true spiritual safety.

"The fountain of Jacob shall be upon a land of corn and wine; also His heavens shall drop down dew." Not merely a land of corn and wine, but a fountain given beside. There was to be plenty of corn and wine in a land where everything was that was necessary. Water also, and dew also from heaven; and all this was given to the Israelites not because they deserved it, but as a token of their Father's love to them. And up to this present day is God thus going on with regard to His children. Everything that they really need, everything that is really good for them, everything that would truly prove a blessing to them, He is ready to give to them. And so, in our case, if the land of corn and wine were a blessing to us, it would be given to us; whatever is a real, true blessing God bestows, God delights to bestow, on His children. It is the very joy of His heart to do them good, at all times and under all circumstances; and He not only is willing to give them, where there is plenty of corn and wine, and plenty of water, but He also is ready to give them the dew in addition to these, so that everything may be there that tends to fruitfulness. All this for the purpose of making them as happy as they are capable of being while yet in the body.

Now, the result of all this. "Happy art thou, O Israel; who is like unto thee, O people saved by the Lord, the shield of thy help, and who is the sword of thy excellency; and thine enemies shall be found liars unto thee, and thou shalt tread upon their high places." "Happy art thou, O Israel." Now, the solemn, momentous question here is, "Are we happy?" We should individually ask ourselves at this moment, "Am I happy? Am I truly happy? Spiritually happy?" Not merely, "Have I enough of the necessaries of life?" Not merely, "Have I enough so that I am not at present in great trouble and difficulty?" But, "Am I spiritually happy?" That is the momentous point; and this real, true happiness is alone to be obtained through faith in Christ. We have to own before God that we are sinners, deserving no happiness; we have to own before God, that we are sinners, deserving nothing but punishment; and then to put our trust alone in Jesus Christ for the salvation of our souls. This brings about spiritual happiness. At first it may be only in a small degree; but the more we ponder what God has done for us in Christ, the more we feed spiritually on the Lord Jesus Christ, the more this peace and joy in God will increase. But there must be, first of all, a beginning made; and the question therefore is, "Have I the beginning of real, true, happiness in my soul? Do I know the Lord Jesus Christ? Have I come to Him for the salvation of my soul? Do I simply look to Him for salvation?" For without this, there is no real, true happiness to be had!

"Happy art thou, O Israel; who is like unto thee, O people saved by the Lord?" Are we saved by the Lord? That means, in other words, Do we comply with the conditions which God lays down in His Holy Word to save people? Do we put our trust in Jesus for the salvation of our souls? In doing so, the end will be peace and joy and happiness in a little degree; and the more we live on Christ, the more this real, true peace, joy, and happiness will increase. "Who is like unto thee, O people saved by the Lord?" Who among us is able to say, "I am saved by the Lord; if the Lord Jesus were to come round, I should be found a saved one; if the Lord Jesus should take me now out of the world I am a saved one?" Who among us is able to say this? By the grace of God I am one of those who are able to say it; and it is just this which makes me truly happy. Without knowing this, there is no such thing as real, true happiness. "O people saved by the Lord!" Then of Jehovah it is further said, "He is the Shield of thy help." He protects us. The shield was particularly for the sake of warding off the blows of the sword, or the power to harm of the dart; therefore the shield was used to protect. And so, for our protection, we are spiritually shielded, and God Himself is the shield.

"Who is the sword of thy excellency." That is true! It is God Himself Who is our sword, power, might, strength, and no accidents will come to us. It is not by our sword. It is not by our power, but by the arm of God, the power of God; and Him we have for us. He is on our side, and throughout eternity He will be on our side, if we are believers in the Lord Jesus Christ. "And thine enemies shall be found liars unto thee." That is, shall be overturned, overthrown, conquered, shall have no power over thee, but thou shalt have power over them. "And thou shalt tread upon their high places"--that is, shalt drive them out, shalt overpower them, shalt overcome them. In their high places they make their boast; but thou shalt take their high places, and conquer them.

Now, once more, the great point is to know Christ, to be a believer in Him, to be found in Him. Now by far the greater part of those here present have found Him, and are believers in the Lord Jesus. Still there are a few present who are not yet believers in the Lord Jesus; and, therefore, real, true happiness and safety are not found as yet in them. But they may secure the like happiness which we who are believers in Jesus Christ have obtained. For we did not give it to ourselves, it was not by our goodness, merit, and worthiness that we came to what we have come, but by the mercy of God, through the grace of God, through faith in Jesus Christ wrought in us by the power of the Holy Ghost. And just as we, in the way of grace, obtained this blessing so any, in the way of grace also, may obtain a like blessing. No one has to say, "I am too far from God." They cannot be! "I am too great a sinner." This cannot be! Because there is power in the blood of the Lord Jesus Christ over all sin; and every sin of which we have been guilty may be forgiven us through faith in the Lord Jesus Christ. O, how precious that no one need despair!

Everyone who seeks salvation in God's own appointed way, that is by alone resting on Christ for salvation, after they have confessed to being sinners, will obtain the blessing. But if in the least degree we depend upon ourselves, and think that we have to save ourselves, or to do something in order that we may be saved, we are holding a grievous error, and we shall never obtain the blessing. By the mercy of God, through faith in Jesus Christ, the oldest sinner, the greatest sinner, may obtain blessing; and, therefore, no one need despair as to the salvation of his soul. Let us go hence, if we are not believers in the Lord Jesus Christ, under the deep conviction that we, individually, may obtain the blessing, and that there is nothing to hinder us. Once the blessing is obtained, little by little we shall be led on, by the grace of God, and by the help of God's Holy Spirit. God grant us individually a blessing according to our need.

Chapter 7: The Lost Sheep, The Lost Piece of Silver, The Prodigal Son.

A Sermon preached at Bethesda Chapel, Great George Street, Bristol, on Sunday Evening, July 4th, 1897.

Luke 15.

WE WILL READ the whole chapter, and on some of the verses we will meditate, as the Lord may help us. "Then drew near unto Him all the publicans and sinners for to hear Him." This is particularly to be noticed. Two classes especially sought to hear the Lord Jesus-"sinners," that is, notorious sinners, who lived in gross immorality, and who came because they wanted something for their souls; and "publicans," those officers who were noted for defrauding those with whom they had to do. These two classes, particularly, came by reason of their spiritual wants. "And the Pharisees and Scribes murmured, saying, 'This man receiveth sinners and eateth with them.'" These individuals were self-righteous persons, who had, generally speaking, a very high opinion of themselves, who thought themselves far better than others, and who looked down upon other classes of persons, especially on the publicans and on those who were known as notorious sinners. On this account, because they were self-righteous, they murmured. If they had really been God-fearing persons, they would have rejoiced that these "publicans and sinners" sought to hear the Lord Jesus, because there was the prospect of their being benefited through hearing Him.

But self-righteousness is connected with pride and high-mindedness, and so they murmured and said, "This man receiveth sinners." So He does! And If He did not, we should all be lost. Salvation would not be possible if the Lord Jesus Christ did not "receive sinners," because all human beings since Adam and Eve belong to a fallen race, all were unfit to save themselves, all were not in a state of getting to Heaven, except they obtained a Substitute on their account, and that Substitute was the Lord Jesus Christ. And instead of rejoicing that the Lord Jesus received sinners, the Scribes and Pharisees murmured. They were dissatisfied, whereas they ought to have been grateful. For all their good opinions about themselves, they needed a Saviour as much as these publicans.

"And He spake this parable unto them." How came it that the Lord Jesus spake this parable to them? Because He knew what was passing in their hearts, and in what state they were. "He spake this parable unto them, saying, 'What man of you, having an hundred sheep, if he lose one of them, doth not leave the ninety and nine in the wilderness, and go after that which is lost until he find it? And when he hath found it, he layeth it on his shoulders rejoicing, and when he cometh home he calleth together his friends and neighbours, saying unto them, "Rejoice with me for I have found my sheep which was lost."'" By this shepherd is represented our Lord Jesus Christ, the "Great Shepherd of the sheep," the "Chief Shepherd;" and the love which He has to poor sinners is set forth in the parable. When we, who are believers in Christ, look at ourselves, we are compelled to say, "This is just my case; my Lord Jesus Christ has been looking after me in the past of my life, in a variety of ways, seeking me, caring about my soul, and leaving me not until He has found me." Is not this the case with everyone of us? We had cared nothing about God, we went our own way, we sought to please ourselves, to gratify ourselves, one in this way, another in that way; one in the pride of life," another in "the lust of the eyes," and another in "the lust of the flesh." But in whatever way we sought joy and happiness, it was in a way which was contrary to the mind of God; and the Lord Jesus Christ knocked at our heart's door in a variety of ways, by this trial, by that trial; by this disappointment, by that disappointment; by this loss, by that loss; and so He sought after us, and gave us not up until He had brought us to Himself.

Further, the one lost sheep is here particularly dwelt on, not that the others were not also loved and cared for; but so great is the love of the Lord Jesus Christ to any and every poor sinner who as yet does not know Him, that He goes on seeking, seeking, seeking, till He has found him. O, how precious! Now there may be two or three, peradventure even more, here present regarding whom this is the case. I have reason to believe that it is God's especial purpose that I should bring this chapter before some such. It is most remarkable that while I have preached tens of thousands of times within the last seventy-one years, in the case of this particular chapter, which is so often spoken about, and from which so frequently texts are taken, I have never once before in my life preached! I call it a very remarkable circumstance. Yesterday, again and again I bowed my knees before the Lord to teach me what subject I should speak about this evening. I had no subject laid on my heart. Even during the night, while I was awake, I asked God to guide and direct me. I had no text when I got up. Then, before the meeting this morning, I again and again asked God to show me on what I should preach to-night. No text yet, and this afternoon again I cried to God to teach me, when all at once this passage was impressed upon my mind.

Now, I reckon this to be a remarkable circumstance. The many scores of times that I have read this portion, at least one hundred and fifty times, since my conversion, without having been led to speak upon it, is an indication in my own mind that God means to knock, by the power of His Spirit, at the heart of someone or other here present. Now, let such who as yet know not the Lord Jesus Christ say to themselves, " Is Mr. Muller directed to this chapter for my sake?" "Does it not become me to pay attention?" "Is not the Lord by His Spirit knocking at my heart, through the instrumentality of this chapter, and is it not high time that I surrender my heart to Him, that I own that I am a sinner, that I acknowledge before God in prayer that I deserve nothing but punishment, and that I began to put my trust alone in Jesus Christ, the Saviour of sinners, because He fulfilled the commandments which I have broken times without number, and bore the punishment in order that I might escape?" Thus those here present, who as yet know not the Lord, Jesus is going after you, my fellow-sinner, in order to save you. That is the reason. If He wished that you should be destroyed, He would let you alone and care nothing at all about you; but this is the very reverse regarding the Lord Jesus. He delights to save sinners, and, therefore, He goes after them until He finds them. All those here present who know the Lord know how He went after them till He found them.

Then see the tenderness of this precious Saviour. "When He hath found it He layeth it on His shoulders." Just think what this figure means. That the sheep might not be troubled or hurt by walking, that all the danger in the way might count as nothing He carries the sheep. O, the love of this Saviour! The tenderness of His heart is brought afresh before us in this parable. Then, further, He does this rejoicing, rejoicing. Though the sinner may not care about his sin, yet not merely does the Saviour seek after the sinner; but when He finally finds him, and brings him to himself, He does so rejoicing, because it is the delight of His heart to make us happy, and He knows that while we are going our own way, we cannot possibly be happy.

"And when he cometh home he calleth together his friends and neighbours saying unto them, 'Rejoice with me for I have found my sheep which was lost.' I say unto you that likewise joy shall be in heaven over one sinner that repenteth more than over ninety and nine just persons which need no repentance." Here we find something particularly to be noticed. "Joy in heaven," on the part of the redeemed, on the part of the holy, unfallen angels; all the hosts in heaven rejoicing when they hear that another soul has been won for our Lord Jesus Christ. Now, any here present who are as yet strangers to this great salvation, will you not give joy to Jesus by surrendering your heart to God? Will you not give joy in heaven to the elect angels, the holy angels, and to the redeemed by yielding your heart to the Lord Jesus?

"Either what woman having ten pieces of silver, if she lose one piece, doth not light a candle, and sweep the house, and seek diligently till she find it? And when she hath found it, she calleth her friends and her neighbours together, saying, 'Rejoice with me, for I have found the piece which I had lost.' Likewise, I say unto you, there is joy in the presence of the angels of God over one sinner that repenteth."

"And He said, 'A certain man had two sons, and the younger of them said to his father, "Father, give me the portion of goods that falleth to me;" and he divided unto them his living ' " (that is, his possession) " 'and not many days after, the younger son gathered all together, and took his journey into a far country, and there wasted his substance with riotous living. And when he had spent all, there arose a mighty famine in that land, and he began to be in want; and he went and joined himself to a citizen of that country, and he sent him into his fields to feed swine. And he would fain have filled his belly with the husks that the swine did eat, and no man gave unto him.'" This younger son asked his father to give him the property which, in the case of the death of the parent, was coming to him; to give it to him while he (the father) was yet living. Now, the father was not obliged to do this, but he did it, showing real, true love to the son.

But how did the son treat him, as soon as he was in possession? Without waiting any length of time, only a few days, after he had come into the possession of the property, "he gathered all together, and took his journey into a far country." Going away from his father, from his kind father, from his loving father. And that is just the way in which we, in our unconverted state, treat God. We do not abide in His presence. We cannot bear His presence, because naturally we are wicked; we go our own way; we wish to please ourselves; we wish to do the things which are hateful to God. And because of this we leave Him, and go from Him.

Then, after he had left his father, and gone into a far country, this son, having now no one to look after him, to care about him, and to admonish him, "wasted his substance with riotous living," just carrying out his natural evil propensities to the utmost. "And when he had spent all, there arose a mighty famine in that land, and he began to be in want." Now, the description which is given here brings before us, spiritually, the real, true condition-the miserable, wretched condition-in which we are as long as we are not believers in the Lord Jesus Christ. The sinner, who is not a believer is to the very utmost in spiritual want; he has no Father in heaven, he has no Saviour, he has no Holy Spirit dwelling in him, and he is not admonished by the Word of God, because he cares nothing at all about that Word, he has no fellowship with the children of God. All this is wanting, and, therefore, he is really and truly spiritually in want, though he may have plenty of money, plenty of worldly friends, plenty of the possessions of this life,

"And he went and joined himself to a citizen of that country." Now, what does the citizen of that country do for him? He does not say, "O, my friend, I have much feeling for you; come to my house and live with me, and share with me everything that I have; I will try to make you as comfortable as I can!" Nothing of the kind. The description here given brings before us the wretchedness, the misery, the real, true wretchedness and misery we feel as long as we are without Christ. The citizen sends him into his fields to feed swine. Naturally, irrespective of his being an Israelite, a most wretched occupation this, "to feed swine;" but to him, who was born an Israelite, it was doubly and trebly and tenfold a trial. Therefore, I say, this brings before us the wretchedness and misery in which the sinner is as long as he is without Christ. Then, further, we read, "He would fain have filled his belly with the husks that the swine did eat." This, the most miserable and wretched food, the food of unclean animals, this he would have gladly have eaten, if he could have had it, but he could not. "No man gave unto him."

Now comes the turning point. "And when he came to himself, he said, 'How many hired servants of my father's have bread enough and to spare, and I perish with hunger!' " "When he came to himself; " that is, pondered his ways. He saw then what had befallen him, in consequence of the manner in which he had been acting towards his father by leaving him and wasting his property in the way he had. "He came to himself." Now, I affectionately ask all here present, "Have we individually, without an exception, come to ourselves?" By the grace of God, I have come to myself, and by the grace of God, there are many scores here present who have come to themselves; they have pondered their ways, they have seen that they are sinners; they have found out that if they continued in the way in which they were going on, it would have ended in misery and wretchedness for ever and ever. And if that is not to be the case, we all must come to ourselves, and the sooner we do so the better. Therefore, again I ask affectionately this question, "Have we individually come to ourselves? Have we individually found out the evil way in which we are going on? And that, if we continue in this state, it must end in perdition, in wretchedness and misery to the end?" "When he came to himself, he said, 'How many hired servants of my father's have bread enough and to spare, and I perish with hunger! I will arise and go to my father, and will say unto him, "Father, I have sinned against heaven, and before thee, and am no more worthy to be called thy son; make me as one of thy hired servants." ' "

Now, to some such decision we have to come; we have not merely to ponder and consider our ways, but we have to decide to forsake them, to come to God, to humble ourselves before Him, to own that we are sinners, that we deserve nothing but punishment, and then to put our trust in the Lord Jesus Christ alone for salvation. This is the way in which we have to act, and this is the way which will bring blessing to the soul. "I will arise," he says, " and go to my father." So must we say to ourselves. And he not merely purposed to do it, but he actually did do it. That is the special point we have to notice in the 20th verse, "And he arose, and came to his father." He did not say, "I am shabbily dressed, I am so wretchedly miserable, I am ashamed to go to my father." Nothing of the sort. "My sins have been too great, and too many, and too varied; therefore, I am ashamed to go to him." No. Conscious of all this in himself, "he arose, and came to his father."

Thus we have actually to turn to God, and the result or it will be blessedness, eternal blessedness and happiness; and the reception that we shall meet with on the part of our Father, our Heavenly Father, will be of the most loving, tender character. "When he was yet a great way off, his father saw him, and had compassion, and ran, and fell on his neck, and kissed him." This brings before us the heart of our Heavenly Father, for if an earthly father would act in that way, by reason of his love to a son, O, how much more abundantly would this be true regarding our Heavenly Father in His love to us poor sinners. The father did not say, " This, my son, has given me great sorrow, great trouble, I have wept many times on his account. Now, I will let him who has given me such sorrow come to me; I will not go a step to meet him." Nothing of the kind. "When he saw him yet a great way off, he had compassion on him, and ran." O, think of this! How it brings before us the heart of God. "And fell on his neck, and kissed him." Before the son who had given him such sorrow, such pain, and had so deeply wounded him, had uttered a single word, he fell on his neck, and kissed him. O, how precious! All this brings before us our Heavenly Father; all these figures tell us of what we have in God, and what we have in our Lord Jesus Christ.

"And the son said unto him, 'Father, I have sinned against heaven, and in thy sight, and am no more worthy to be called thy son.' But the father said to his servants, 'Bring forth the best robe and put it on him; and put a ring on his hand, and shoes on his feet, and bring hither the fatted calf, and kill it; and let us eat and be merry, for this, my son, was dead, and is alive again, he was lost and is found;' and they began to be merry." Not a single word of reproof, but love, love, love, the manifestation of love. And nothing but a manifestation of love is what we meet with from our Heavenly Father in reference to ourselves. That is what we are taught by this parable, and in the figures which are used. "The father said to his servants, 'Bring forth the best robe.' " The best robe that was to be had in the house, that was in his possession-that was put on him. Now, we have also, spiritually, the best robe put on us-"The Robe of Righteousness." All they who put their trust in the Lord Jesus Christ, from the moment that they do so, are no more looked on by God as they are in themselves, but as they are in Christ, for He in our room and stead, fulfilled the law of God, and this becomes "the best robe" that we could have. The filthy rags of our own righteousness are removed, and this best robe, the comeliness of Christ, the perfection of Jesus, the justification we have through faith in Him, is put on us.

"And put a ring on his hand." Gave it to him; indicating what we receive as believers in Christ. We obtain the Spirit. Thus are we regenerated, born again, become the children of God, and, as such, the heirs of God and joint-heirs with Christ. O, what precious things are given to us by coming to the Lord Jesus Christ! "And shoes on his feet." When we come to the Lord Jesus Christ, and return spiritually to our Heavenly Father, we obtain not merely full forgiveness for all our numberless transgressions, but we also obtain the help that we require to walk to the praise, and honour, and glory of God, which is set forth by the shoes on our feet, for the way is rough and difficult. But we obtain help from God to be able to walk in it.

"And bring hither the fatted calf, and kill it, and let us be merry." This also is particularly to be noticed-the joy that we can give to God Himself. Though He is the Almighty God, and the Infinitely Wise One, yet we can give joy even to Him, by turning from our evil ways and going back to Him. And this is set forth by the fatted calf being killed, and all eating and making merry, rejoicing, because the lost son had been brought back. "For this, my son, was dead and is alive again, he was lost and is found; and they began to be merry." Now, this very evening, some can thus give great joy to God by surrendering their hearts to Him, by owning that they are sinners, that they deserve nothing but punishment, and by putting their trust now, simply and solely, in the Lord Jesus Christ for salvation. Thus they can give joy to the heart of God, and joy to the heart of the Lord Jesus, and joy to the Spirit; and joy to the holy angels and the redeemed in glory.

"Now, his elder son was in the field, and as he came and drew nigh to the house, he heard music and dancing; and he called one of the servants, and asked what these things meant, and he said unto him, 'Thy brother is come, and thy father hath killed the fatted calf, because he hath received him safe and sound; , and he was angry, and would not go in. Therefore, came his father out and entreated him." Precious! Precious! O, what a heart is found in Him! For this again sets forth the heart of God! The tenderness, the loveliness, the kindness, on the part of this earthly father represents to us, in figure, what we, who are believers in Christ, have obtained in God. The brother was a self-righteous person, and behaved shamefully. Because his brother had lived in open sin, he considered himself far superior to him, and hated him-for it is nothing but a real, true hatred that is manifested here. "And as he came and drew nigh to the house, he heard music and dancing," and on receiving the answer as to what it meant, he was angry. Just manifesting the same kind of spirit as the prophet Jonah, when Nineveh not being destroyed, as he wished it, was angry, was displeased with God.

And now hear how the father dealt with this elder son. Because he was angry, on account of the manner in which his brother had been received, "He would not go in." O, what a sad state of heart! It shows to us what it is to be in a self-righteous condition. It is one of the most pernicious things we could fall into." Therefore came his father out, and intreated him! " O, the loveliness of such a father! "And he answering said to his father, 'Lo, these many years do I serve thee, neither transgressed I at any time thy commandement.'" He was, indeed, at this very moment transgressing his father's commandment, because his father wished him to go in, and he would not! "And yet thou never gavest me a kid, that I might make merry with my friends; but as soon as this, thy son, was come, which hath devoured thy living with harlots, thou hast killed for him the fatted calf." And he said unto him, "Son, thou art ever with me, and all that I have is thine." In other words, "There is a different state of things, between thee and thy brother; thy brother was considered as being dead, as being lost, and that we should never see him again, but 'thou art ever with me, and all that I have is thine.' I am not merely willing to give to thee a kid, but I am willing to give thee ever so much. If thou hadst asked me, thou wouldst have known how willing I was to give thee a kid."

"It was meet that we should make merry, and be glad; for this, thy brother, was dead and is alive again, and was lost and is found." That is the reason why they were so joyous, because it was considered he was dead, that he was lost. Now, what will be the end of our meditation? The Holy Spirit has been knocking at the hearts of some, and the Lord Jesus Christ is standing before them now, and says, "Will you not let me in? I am your friend, I love you tenderly, I wish to do you good, and to make you very, very happy, not merely for a time, but for eternity, if you will only have me, if you will only let me come into your heart!" Now, what is your reply?

Any here present who have not the Lord Jesus Christ dwelling in them, will you not surrender your heart to the Lord? O, come! Come! Come to Him! Come to Him! I know, from my own experience, the wretchedness and misery that are got by walking in the ways of this world. I sought happiness in the things of this life; but I never found it! Never! Never! All that I met with was disappointment and increased guilt on the conscience; but at last, in the riches of the grace of God, I found Jesus, and immediately I became a happy young man, and I have now been a happy man seventy-one years and eight months. And this happiness which I have received through faith in the Lord Jesus, through surrendering my heart to Him, I do not wish to keep to myself; I delight that others might have the same blessing, and, therefore, I speak as I do. Be sure of this, all who know not Jesus, that real, true happiness, can only be found through faith in Christ. This world cannot give it. Nothing that we can have in this present world can afford us real, true, lasting happiness. That is alone to be found through faith in Christ. Therefore, let no one put it off to the last, but come to Jesus now!

Chapter 8: To Save Sinners.

A Sermon preached at Bethesda Chapel, Great George Street, Bristol, on Sunday Evening, April 4th, 1897.

. - *1 Timothy 1:15, 16.*

THE FIRST POINT we have to consider in these verses is this, that the statement of God the Holy Spirit that Christ came into the world to save sinners is a faithful saying. That implies there is not a shadow of doubt regarding the fact that "Christ Jesus came into the world to save sinners." The matter is as certain as that the earth is in existence. The matter is as certain as that God invariably speaks the truth, and nothing but the truth. It is declared in the Word of God, given by inspiration; that is, written under the immediate power of God the Holy Spirit-therefore it is without a shadow of doubt. And we who are believers in the Lord Jesus Christ should again and again, while life is continued to us here on earth, seek to sound it out far and wide, as much as we possibly can, that it is an entirely correct, perfectly true statement that "Christ Jesus came into the world to save sinners."

The second point regarding this is, that the statement deserves to be accepted. It is "worthy of all acception" we read. And we have, therefore, to ask ourselves regarding the first, Do we believe the statement that "Christ Jesus came into the world to save sinners?" Secondly, Have we in heart received this statement, which God the Holy Spirit makes by the Apostle Paul-for on receiving it, or not receiving it, depends the salvation of our souls! O let us not lightly treat it! Let us not simply read it and speak about it, and have certain notions regarding it; let us not be satisfied until in our inmost souls we have received the statement really and truly that "Christ Jesus came into the world to save sinners."

Then the next point we have to weigh regarding our text is this, it is not stated that Christ Jesus was born into the world to save sinners-though had it been thus stated it would have been perfectly true, for, in reference to His humanity, the Lord Jesus Christ was born into the world. But here His humanity merely not referred to, but more particularly by the statement that "He came into the world to save sinners," His divinity is alluded to, His existence before He was seen on earth. Then He existed, for He is the Creator of the universe, the Upholder of the universe, and He existed from eternity, for He had no beginning of days. This is the particular point, that we have to lay to heart here-that He came into the world to save sinners.

And this brings before us a deeply important truth, regarding which all believers in the Lord Jesus should be clearly, distinctly instructed. In the Messiah, in the Saviour of sinners, in Christ, was united both the human and the divine nature. He was really and truly a man, like ourselves, sin only excepted There was never found a single sin, as to action, nor as to word, nor as to thought, in our Lord Jesus Christ. He ate and drank, He slept, really and truly slept like ourselves, was altogether human like ourselves, sin only in every way most perfectly excepted. It was necessary that He should be really and truly human, in order that in our room and stead, by perfectly fulfilling the law, He might work out a righteousness in which we could be accepted before God, through faith in His Name. For this very reason, it was necessary that He should be human like ourselves, that He should come under the Law, that He might fulfil the Law, and thus bring in everlasting righteousness to the poor sinner who trusts in Him. So that we, on account of Christ, could be reckoned righteous on the part of God. This is most precious, and we have to ponder it again and again, and to see clearly and distinctly that we may have full comfort under the deep consciousness of our manifold failures and shortcomings.

Further, it was absolutely needful that He should be truly human like ourselves, sin only excepted, in order that, as a human being, He might feel, really and truly feel, the punishment which came on Him as our Substitute. Had the Saviour been only divine, and not truly human also, He would not have felt the pain and the suffering while passing on through this vale of tears for thirty-three years and a half, and especially when He hung on the Cross, when His precious hands and precious feet were pierced through with large nails, and when He shed His blood for the remission of our sins. O how deeply important it is to consider all this!

Then, lastly, it was needful that He should be truly human, sin only excepted, in order that, as our Great High Priest, He might feel sympathy for us, in our trials, in our sufferings, in our pain, and in our need. For these reasons, then, it was necessary that the Saviour of sinners should be truly human. But this is only one side of the truth. The other side is that He was at the same time as really and truly divine as the Father! This was perfectly needful, in order that, in the first place, He might be able to endure all that which came on Him, in connection with the hour of darkness. A mere human being, though perfectly holy, perfectly sinless, could not have been able to endure all these pains, and torments, and agonies, which were brought on Him, when, as our Substitute, He bore the punishment, which we deserved, for our numberless transgressions. For this reason it was absolutely needful that the Saviour of sinners should be divine, as well as human.

It was further necessary that He should be divine in order to give value to His precious blood, for by it not merely one sinner was to be saved, not merely a thousand sinners, not merely a million sinners, but an innumerable company. Therefore this must be the blood of the God Man, Christ Jesus, not merely the blood of the man, Christ Jesus, not merely the blood of the One, Who had been born at Bethlehem by the Virgin Mary, and brought up at Nazareth as an ordinary man, but the God-Man, the Creator of the universe, the Upholder of the universe. And thus, because of His being really and truly God, power was given to that blood shed for the remission of our sins, to save an innumerable multitude! O how precious the consideration of this, that we may have full consolation in the fact that He Who died on the cross shed the blood of the God-Man, a the blood of God," as it is stated in the 28th verse of the 20th chapter of the Acts of the Apostles.

Lastly, it was necessary that He should be truly divine, in order that the powers of darkness might not have the ability of overthrowing the atoning work which our precious Lord Jesus began on earth, and is carrying on now in glory. Had He, our Substitute, been merely human, though the most holy and spotless of human beings, the devils would have sought opportunity, without hesitating one moment, to overturn this atoning work of His; but because the atoning work was commenced and is carried on by One Who is really God, Satan, who is a mere creature, cannot overturn the work. Therefore, the salvation of our souls is certain. Now, may the beloved young disciples particularly seek to clearly understand the necessity of the true humanity of our Lord, and the true divinity, as being absolutely needful regarding the salvation of our souls.

The next point we have to ponder is that, "He came into the world to save sinners." This word is full of comfort in particular. O what would have become of all who are believers in Christ were there not this statement. Had it been stated, "He came into the world to save good people, who needed something of His help; excellent people, who were not completely perfect, and needed a little of His help!" O, then, what would have become of great sinners like myself? We should have no comfort. But it is simply stated, "He came into the world to save sinners." Therefore none are excluded, whether they are young sinners, or old sinners, whether they have been guilty of many sins or few sins! No exception made here! "He came into the world to save sinners." That implies even the oldest sinners, the most notorious sinners, the most hardened sinners; those who have been guilty times without number, those whose sins are more in number than the hairs of their head. Even such can be saved by Him. O how precious! O how precious! No poor sinner is excluded, provided he seeks salvation in God's appointed way, through the Lord Jesus Christ. O unspeakably blessed this!

Now what have we to do on our part, in order to partake of the benefit of what the Lord Jesus Christ has done, as our Substitute, is first to see the need of a Saviour. There are many people who think themselves very good, very excellent people, who look on the drunkard, the thief, and the robber with utter contempt, because they regard themselves as such very good and excellent people. They trust that by their good life and excellent deportment they will get to heaven, not knowing that, by our own strength, we can only fit ourselves for hell. But of the thousands upon thousands, the tens of thousands upon tens of thousands that have been on earth since the creation, there has not been one single individual ever found who by his own goodness and merit and worthiness, brought himself to heaven. On the other hand, numberless individuals, by their own goodness and merit, have brought themselves to hell, to perdition, because they trusted in their own goodness, instead of trusting in Christ.

Therefore the first thing, in order to partake of this salvation prepared by the Lord Jesus Christ for poor sinners is that we see, clearly and distinctly see, we need a Saviour, that we cannot save ourselves by our own goodness, merit, and worthiness. In the Word of God, our own righteousness is compared to filthy rags, and God will have no filthy rags in heaven. Clean, fine, white linen, spotlessness, He requires for His own presence. I repeat, therefore, the first thing, if we desire to be saved through Jesus Christ, is that we see we are sinners, that we see we need a Saviour, and that we put our trust in Him alone for salvation. If we cannot see this, we should ask God to show it to us, and should read His Word, in which it is plainly stated -for instance, in the first three chapters of the Epistle of Paul to the Romans, and in the second chapter of the Epistle to the Ephesians, besides a number of other portions-that all human beings, without exception, are sinners. Then when we see it, we have to confess before God that we are sinners, deserving punishment; and have to ask Him that He would be pleased, by the power of His Holy Spirit, to help us to put our trust alone in Jesus for the salvation of our souls. Thus is brought to us peace and joy in God; and the more we enter into it, the more clearly we see it and apprehend it, the greater will be the peace and joy in our souls. After the Apostle Paul had made this statement, that "Christ Jesus came into the world to save sinners," he adds, "of whom I am chief." This not merely carelessly or in a flippant way uttered. Nothing of the kind! This is his sure and hearty conviction, that he was the greatest sinner, that he was the chief of sinners, for he could never forget that he had been so great a persecutor of the Church of God, that he had again and again and again beaten the believers in Christ, that he had cast them into prison, that he had worried them until at last they blasphemed the Name of Jesus-at least he had aimed at it, and would not let them go till he had done his utmost to make them do so-and then, lastly, whenever he possibly could, he had sought to see that they were put to death. Now, on account of all this, which he never could forget and which he refers to again and again in his epistles, and in the Acts of the Apostles, he calls himself "the chief of sinners." We, in a thoughtless and flippant way, may use the same expression; but we should lay it to heart that thus it was not with the Apostle Paul. He meant what he said in calling himself, " the chief of sinners."

But this is only one side of it! Here comes the other side. He obtained forgiveness, pardon. "Howbeit for this cause I obtained mercy, that in me, first, Jesus Christ might show forth all long-suffering, for a pattern to them which should hereafter believe on Him to life everlasting." The first thing we have to observe regarding this second verse of our text is, that the Apostle Paul knew he was a forgiven sinner, a pardoned sinner. Now, how is it with ourselves regarding this point? I am now particularly referring to believers. If we are believers in the Lord Jesus, do we know that we are forgiven ones? Do we know that everyone of our sins is forgiven? That not a single sin shall be brought against us hereafter, if we are believers in the Lord Jesus Christ? That, therefore, the one only hateful thing which stands between the sinner and his God, that is sin itself, is put aside? That in the sight of God, we are clean ones, spotless ones, holy ones, because we are forgiven ones. O how precious!

I walk up and down in my room in prayer and in meditation about the things of God; I come out before God with this sin and with another sin, with very many sins of which I have been guilty, and which God the Holy Spirit brings to my remembrance! But it is always wound up with "These, my numberless transgressions, are forgiven!" Every one of my sins forgiven! Not a single sin remains unforgiven! Therefore I am completely reconciled to God, and God reconciled to me! O how precious! And the result of it all is peace and joy in the Holy Ghost! Not decreased by the remembrance of all our numberless transgressions, but increased more, because we see more clearly God's wondrous love to us in Christ Jesus.

Should there be a single believer present who does not yet know that his sins are all forgiven, completely forgiven, that he has obtained mercy from God, though a sinner, a great sinner, let such a one not give himself rest till he knows it for himself, for there is no lasting peace till we come to know that all our numberless transgressions are forgiven. Let us not say we cannot know this on earth; we must wait till we get to heaven. Nay, the very opposite. It is the will of God that we should know it while we are yet in the body, for He has clearly and distinctly revealed to us that our sins are all forgiven if we are believers in Christ, as it is written in the 43rd verse of the 10th chapter of the Acts of the Apostles regarding the Lord Jesus, "To Him give all the prophets witness, that through His Name whosoever believeth in Him shall receive remission of sins." That is, forgiveness of sins.

By the grace of God. I have known for seventy-one years and five months that all my numberless transgressions are forgiven. I have never had five minutes' doubt about it. And the result has been peace and joy in the Holy Ghost. So it is whenever we are really able to the full to enter into it that all our transgressions are forgiven. We have on no account to say,

"O, here is an Apostle, who writes this; but it is not for us common ordinary believers to know." Everyone of the children of God may know it! Everyone of the children of God ought to know it! Ought to know it, and not give rest to themselves till they know it to the full.

"For this cause I obtained mercy, that in me first." This "first" has a double meaning. Primarily, that a beginning might be laid in his case to be a pattern of the long-suffering of the Lord Jesus Christ; in the next place that in him, the chief of sinners, might be shown what God is willing to do for any and every sinner! Now let us seek to lay hold on this! The Apostle Paul, the great persecutor as he was when he was called Saul, obtained full, complete forgiveness of all the numberless transgressions of which he had been guilty, that a specimen might be given of what the Lord Jesus Christ is willing to do for the oldest, the greatest of all sinners, affording especially a sample in forgiving this vile persecutor of the saints, Saul, in order that no one after him need to despair whether it be possible that he or she could obtain forgiveness of sins. Of the hundreds of millions of human beings now under heaven, it is impossible that there can be one single individual who is too great a sinner to be forgiven; for he (Paul) was forgiven to be a sample that hereafter no one need despair. O this text! How precious! If this building were gold, or were filled with gold, it would be as nothing in comparison with the preciousness of this verse! "Howbeit for this cause I obtained mercy, that in me first"-that in me first- "Jesus Christ might show forth all long-suffering." That is long-suffering to the utmost, a sample of what He is willing to do for any and everyone! "For a pattern"-that is, for an example, for a proof-"to them which should hereafter believe on Him." O, precious! That there might not be, of all the numberless millions of human beings, a single individual who should have Scriptural ground to say, "I am too great a sinner to be pardoned."

Then, lastly, one word more, "Believe on Him to life everlasting." That means to eternal joy and happiness; as "an heir of God, and joint-heir with Christ" to share with Him the glory, and to be unspeakably happy throughout Eternity, by partaking of the rivers of pleasure at the right hand of God. O, ponder, ponder, ponder, again, again, and again, and pray over it yet further and further, what is contained in this word, "Believe on Him to life everlasting." The pleasures of this life, of this world, and the possessions of this world are exposed to change, and all is vanity. It is simply of the world. But what we receive in Christ brings eternal joy, eternal happiness; joy and happiness that will never be taken from us!

O, pray for this yet more and more! Seek to apprehend it more and more, and to lay hold on it further and further, more clearly and distinctly than as yet you have done, my beloved younger brethren and sisters in Christ. God grant it, for His Name's Sake.

Chapter 9: The Resurrection of the Body.

Delivered at Bethesda Chapel, Great George Street, Bristol, October 3rd, 1897.

2 Cor. 5:1.

AS THE LORD may help us, we will meditate on the verses we have now been reading. They particularly refer to the resurrection body, which means the glorified body, that believers in Christ shall have, and in which they shall be seen, at the return of the Lord Jesus Christ, such a body as the Lord Jesus Himself received after His resurrection.

"For we know." This is in connection with what is stated in the last verses of the previous chapter. "For we know that if our earthly house of this tabernacle were dissolved, we have a building of God, a house not made with hands, eternal in the heavens." Our present body is called "an earthly house of this tabernacle." In other words, shortly, briefly, "a tent-house"-that is, our present body is a tent-house. A tent may be broken up, and pitched elsewhere. It may be very soon broken up. Thus it is with regard to the body in which we are now. It is frail, it is weak, it is earthly, it is of time-in contrast with the glorified body which we shall have. No more weakness, no more frailty then; no more of the earthly character, but of the heavenly character! No more of the body of time, but of Eternity. That is the difference between our present bodies and the body we shall have.

"We know that if our earthly house of this tabernacle were dissolved," if this tent-house were dissolved, "we have a building of God." It is likened to a building to bring before us the substantial character, and the enduring character of it, in comparison with a tent. "A house not made with hands, eternal in the heavens." The glorified body we shall receive at the return of the Lord Jesus is eternal; and all weakness, all infirmity, will be done with for ever. No more pain, no more weakness, no more sickness, no more death-all gone completely; gone, all this in connection with our glorified body. And this is something exceedingly refreshing to the inner man. Now those who seek to labour for the Lord in a variety of ways-it may be in the Sunday School, or as tract circulators, as visitors from house to house of the unconverted, or as visitors of the sick, in all these various ways in which they may labour, they may go on for four or five hours, those who are of greater physical strength may be able to go on six or seven hours, it may be even eight hours, but at last the weakness comes, the "being-tired" is felt, and they are obliged to discontinue going on further in the work, and leave it to the next day. All this will be at an end for ever and ever.

There will be labouring in eternity. There will be no sleeping, no folding hands throughout eternity; but work, continual service constrained by the love of Christ. And this working for the Lord, this seeking to glorify Him by our labour, will go on hour after hour, one four-and-twenty hours after the other, one week after the other, one month after the other, one year after the other, one hundred years after the other, one thousand years after the other, one million years after the other, during a period which never, never, never, will come to an end; and the delightful service going on all the time is held out as an especial promise to the Church of God, not merely that the curse will be gone when we are in glory, but an exceedingly high honour and glorious privilege. "His servants shall serve Him," we read at the close of the Book of Revelation. All our work, and labour, and service, much and varied as it may have been while on earth, shall be considered as nothing in comparison with what there will be of work going on throughout eternity. O how precious this consideration in connection with our glorified body. We shall have that without the least particle of weariness; we shall go on labouring for ever and ever to the glory of God!

Therefore this word "eternal" is so precious! "Eternal in the heavens." In the heavens we shall obtain this glorified body. "For in this"-that is, in our present tent-house, in our present frame of weakness, our body of infirmities-"For in this we groan, earnestly desiring to be clothed upon with our house which is from heaven." One groaning on account of weakness; another groaning on account of pain, another groaning on account of other infirmities connected with the tent-house in which we find ourselves at present; but especially on account of spiritual infirmities, spiritual weaknesses. SIN-on account of this the child of God especially groans, longing to be delivered from all the spiritual weaknesses, spiritual infirmities, which even in the best of us are found. For the more holy we are, the more do we find ourselves extremely burdened on account of the spiritual infirmities that yet remain in us. "In this we groan earnestly desiring to be clothed upon with our house which is from heaven." At present we are not "clothed upon" in this life. We have not a glorified body. We are yet in this tent-house"

"If so be that being clothed we shall not be found naked." Do you all understand this verse? Just ask yourselves what we mean to put on, for it is important to understand this verse, and I have reason to consider that some do not know what is the meaning of it. Therefore, with such particularly who have doubts about whether they understand it or not, seek to pay attention to what it means. The time will come when there will be given a glorified body; but will all human beings obtain it? No! There will be the first resurrection, the resurrection of the just, there will be the resurrection when the glorified bodies will be given; but not all human beings will obtain the glorified body; the time of the resurrection will have passed, and multitudes not have obtained a glorified body! O let us see to it that when the time comes that the glorified body shall be given, when the time comes to be clothed, "we shall not be found naked." That is, found to have been left in the grave, found not to have obtained the glorified body; and at the last, at the general resurrection, be raised again but for judgment, not raised again to obtain the glorified body. And regarding all those who do not obtain this glorified body, it is stated here that not being clothed, they shall "be found naked." The time passed of the first resurrection, the resurrection of the just, and the glorified body not obtained! To obtain this, every poor sinner, however feeble and weak spiritually he may be, however ignorant in a variety of ways he may be, yet, if trusting truly in the Lord Jesus Christ, is a child of God, and will obtain a glorified body.

"For we that are in this tabernacle," in this tent-body," do groan, being burdened, not for that we would be unclothed, but clothed upon, that mortality might be swallowed up of life." "We that are in this tabernacle"- that means, we children of God, yet on earth in the ordinary body, in the tent-body-" do groan, being burdened." We cry, we sigh, we wish to be brought to a different state. And what is it that we long for? Not that we should be unclothed; but "clothed upon," to obtain our glorified body, in order that mortality may be "swallowed up of life." This is what the child of God especially longs for, the return of the Lord Jesus Christ-not death, but the return of Christ, because then the whole of the Church of God will obtain; everyone of them, a glorified body, and thus mortality will be "swallowed up of life." For this body that we shall obtain will be an eternal body, and we shall never have to pass through death any more.

"Now He that hath wrought us for the self-same thing is God, Who also hath given unto us the earnest of the Spirit." Notice particularly this precious verse. "He that hath wrought us for the self-same thing." That is, we children of God, weak, feeble, and erring, foolish and ignorant, though as yet we may be, have been appointed for this. God has wrought us for this self-same thing-that we should obtain a glorified body. In other words, I, as assuredly as I am speaking now, shall have a glorified body, and my brethren and sisters in Christ here present, and everyone trusting in Jesus for salvation, will obtain the glorified body. Everyone of us, without exception, for we are appointed for it, we are wrought for it, we are prepared for it, and we have the evidence that it will be so. The earnest is given to us already; and this is, that we have received the Spirit. And as assuredly as we have the Spirit received, so certain is it that we shall have a glorified body. This is the earnest given to us in the gift of the Spirit, to comfort our hearts, to make us look out for this glorified body, to ponder it again and again and again with truth that we shall have a glorified body. For this very purpose was given to us the Holy Spirit, that the Holy Spirit might be the warrant to us to look out for the glorified body.

"Therefore we are always confident"-that is, of good courage-knowing that, whilst we are at home in the body, we are absent from the Lord; for we walk by faith, not by sight. We are confident, I say, and willing rather to be absent from the body, and to be present with the Lord." It would be well that we seek to test ourselves by what is written here. "We are always of good courage, knowing that, whilst we are at home in the body, we are absent from the Lord." That is, we have not yet been brought into the presence of the Lord to have habitual, full, complete communion with Him, and have not entered upon the eternal happiness, as every child of God will have it for ever and ever. "We are confident"-we are of good courage-"I say, and willing rather to be absent from the body, and to be present with the Lord." That means rather wishing that the Lord Jesus Christ would come and take us to Himself than that simply we should die and put off this our tabernacle. Is this the state of our hearts? When we look at ourselves, are we able to say, "We are willing to be absent from the body, and to be present with the Lord; rather to go Home to get our glorified bodies, instead of remaining longer here on earth?" The more we are in a spiritual state, the more this will be the case, but with an exception, one in which Paul found himself, when longing to go home, yet willing to stay longer here on earth to labour for the Lord. With this one exception, the spiritual state of heart is to go home to be with the Lord for ever and ever. But if it pleases God to allow us to labour for Him, to be ready to stay, counting it an honour and privilege to labour yet further on earth. I myself have been praying to obtain the great honour, the glorious privilege to be allowed to stay yet longer in the body, that I might be able, in my weak, feeble measure, to labour further for the Lord, for I count it the greatest honour, the most glorious privilege, to be allowed to do any little thing for my adorable, precious Lord, Who has done so much for me.

"Wherefore we labour, that, whether present or absent, we may be accepted of Him." "We labour" -that is, we endeavour-"that whether present or absent"-that is, whether in the body or out of the body, whether with the Lord or whether from the Lord, that however it may be with us, on earth, or in heaven-"we may be accepted of Him"-that is, please Him well. That is the one great concern we should have, to please our Lord well, whether by labouring much or little, in easy or trying circumstances, among friends or foes, at home or abroad, on the land or on the sea. However it may be with us, as to our circumstances, that we may please Him well is the one great business of life if we are believers in the Lord. How greatly we should endeavour to do this whilst life is continued!

Now, in conclusion of our subject, the most solemn word comes in our last verse. "For we must all appear before the judgment seat of Christ, that every one may receive the things done in his body, according to that he hath done, whether it be good or bad," The Eye of God is on every human being! The Ear of God hears every word uttered by every human being; and whatever we do, and whatever we say, nothing escapes the Ear or the Eye of our Heavenly Father. According to all this, we have to stand before the judgment seat of Christ. The believers, all who trust in Christ, are pardoned for all they have been doing, for all they have been saying, great and many and varied though their failures and shortcomings may have been. All, all who have condemned themselves, passed sentence on themselves, and believe in the Lord Jesus Christ, are escaping thus the judgment. But if we are not believers in the Lord Jesus, if we are going on thoughtlessly and carelessly and unconcerned about the things of God, or trusting in ourselves for salvation, instead of trusting in the Lord Jesus Christ, or think that by living a different life, we are able to make up for past misconduct, which is a fatal, soul-destroying error-if, in any way, we are not thus found believers in the Lord Jesus Christ, then God is under the necessity, as a Holy God, and as a Just God, of bringing us to an account for all our deeds, for all our words, even for everyone of our thoughts. And O how will it be then, when having thus to appear before the judgment seat of Christ, to receive according to the things done in the body? O how will it be then? May I entreat and beseech all here present, who are yet out of Christ, not to come to this, for they will not be able to answer God one thing out of a thousand; they will not be able to justify themselves regarding their doings, their speaking, their thinking.

Numberless millions will be found out, their evil deeds, their sinful words, their unholy thoughts. And O what will be their condemnation at the last, if they are found without Christ? Therefore, before it be too late, let them hasten to Him for the forgiveness of all their numberless transgressions! May God grant it all for Christ's sake. Amen.

Chapter 10: New Year's Address to Christians.

Delivered at the Gospel Hall, St. Nicholas Road, St. Paul s Bristol,
on Sunday morning, January 9th, 1898.

1 Cor. 5:6,7,8.

WE HAVE BEEN reading in the 12th chapter of the Book of Exodus about the institution of the Passover and what it was; and here in this portion, which I have just now read, we find what we have to understand by the Passover; in itself setting forth in type, and setting forth in figure, our Lord Jesus Christ. We will now go through these verses with the object of seeing their connection with the Lord Jesus Christ.

We will read again, therefore, this portion verse by verse. The Book of Exodus, chapter 12: "And the Lord spake unto Moses and Aaron in the land of Egypt, saying, 'This month shall be unto you the beginning of months; it shall be the first month of the year to you.'" Here we find, in one particular, how the Lord Jesus Christ is referred to in type. The moment the sinner sees that he is a sinner, and condemns himself before God as one who deserves nothing but punishment, and at the same time puts his trust alone in Jesus Christ for the salvation of his soul, he becomes a new creature in Christ Jesus. Through this faith in the Lord Jesus Christ we are regenerated, we are born again, we obtain spiritual life; and therefore become completely different from what we were.

Before that, the sinner lives in sin; he is, as the Scripture calls it, "dead in trespasses and sin," and knows nothing really and truly of God; but when his eyes are opened by the power of God the Holy Spirit, and he sees the wretched, miserable condition in which he has been all his life long, and is made to trust in the Lord Jesus Christ for salvation, a new life begins-that is, a spiritual life begins; he is an altered man altogether. Now this is set forth in figure, in the chapter, by the month in which the Passover lamb was instituted, and was being celebrated. It becomes the first month. A new year begins; the state of things is completely altered when we are brought to believe in Jesus Christ.

The third verse: "Speak ye unto all the congregation of Israel, saying, 'In the tenth day of this month they shall take to them every man a lamb according to the house of their fathers, a lamb for an house.' " Here we have to observe that, on the tenth day, this lamb was to he taken from the flock. It was to be a spotless lamb, a perfect lamb; there was to be no blemish in it, else it was not to be taken for the Passover lamb, because all the animals that were used for offering were to be without blemish. Now, although the lamb was taken on the tenth day, it was only to be slain on the fourteenth day; it was not to be slain on the same day that it was chosen from the flock. There is a meaning in this! The Lord Jesus Christ, when He came into the world, was perfectly holy, perfectly -spotless, perfectly sinless; but He had to stay here thirty-three years, in order that this might be proved, and seen by everybody. The powers of darkness were to see it; and the holy, spotless, elect angels of heaven were to see it; and the godly of human beings were to see it-that He was the perfectly Holy, Spotless One. Therefore He had to stay here for a good while, that this might be proved.

This is set forth by the fact that the lamb was to be a spotless lamb, chosen on the tenth day of the month, that opportunity might be given to see further and further on those days to the fourteenth day that it was spotless. "Speak ye unto all the congregation of Israel, saying, 'On the tenth day of this month they shall take to them every man a lamb, according to the house of their fathers, a lamb for an house.'" "Every man a lamb," that is the household-the head of the family was to choose a lamb! Now, it might happen that there were only five or six in the whole family, possibly only four, and yet they were to gather round the lamb, the whole lamb, nothing short of the lamb. Around the lamb they were to gather; the whole lamb, roasted as it was, was to be brought on the table, and was to be eaten, with the legs, and with the purtenances thereof-that is, the heart, the lungs, and the kidneys. The whole lamb they were to have about them.

Therefore, what was to be done if the family were small? They were to invite the neighbour next to them; not the uncle, or the aunt, or the cousins. But the neighbour next to them was to be invited, with his family, in order that there might be sufficient persons for the consumption of the lamb. Now this is very remarkable. It shows to us that they were to live till the Passover time came again in peace! It was a very awful thing if they were to quarrel with their next neighbour; then to invite him to come. This indicates that it was expected that they who gathered around the lamb were living in peace. Now this is just how it should be in the heavenly family. Those who feed on the work of the Lord Jesus Christ should be on good terms with their next-door neighbour; not on good terms only with their uncle, or aunt, or their cousins, but with their next-door neighbour. The whole heavenly family should be altogether on good terms, not merely with the rich among themselves, and the poor among themselves, but all, rich and poor alike, no matter whatever their position in life, whatever the amount of education they have had. As assuredly as we belong to Christ, we should love one another, and we should be on good terms with our neighbours. The question should not be, "Is this one an educated person, or a rich person?" but "Does he or she belong to Christ?" "Does he or she love the Lord Jesus Christ?" That is the point; and then, if such be the case, we should love one another as brethren and sisters in the

Lord Jesus Christ. A very, very instructive point that the next-door neighbour was to come in, and make up the number of those to eat the lamb.

"If the household be too little for the lamb, let him and his neighbour next unto his house take it, according to the number of the souls, every man according to his eating shall make your count for the lamb. Your lamb shall be without blemish [as all the sacrifices are to be], a male of the first year; ye shall take it out from the sheep, or from the goats." "A male of the first year." This is the stronger, and this in type sets forth the Divinity of the Lord Jesus Christ. He was really and truly *A Man*, sin only excepted; but at the same time He was really and truly GOD, as the Father. "Ye shall take it out from the sheep, or from the goats and ye shall keep it up until the fourteenth day of the same month."

"And the whole assembly of the congregation of Israel shall kill it in the evening." This is particularly to be noticed. It is not that merely certain persons need the Lord Jesus Christ, and that ether persons can do without Him! No one will go to heaven without Christ! No one is a real, true believer, except he puts his sole trust for salvation in the Lord Jesus Christ! This is set forth by the fact that "the whole assembly of the congregation of Israel shall kill it in the evening." They all have a part in connection with the Passover, and as assuredly as we are believers in Christ, so surely do we trust in the Death, in the Atonement, of the Lord Jesus Christ; and whosoever does not put his sole, and whole, trust in the Lord Jesus Christ for salvation, does not believe in Christ, and therefore is yet in his sins.

"And they shall take of the blood, and strike it on the two side posts and on the upper door post of the houses, wherein they shall eat it; and they shall eat the flesh in that night, roast with fire." It was not to be eaten raw, nor was it to be eaten sodden with water, but "roast with fire." This brings before us in type the fact that the Lord Jesus Christ was exposed to the wrath of God, that not merely nominally, but really and truly, He had to pass through all the agonies, the torments, the sufferings through which we ought to have passed on account of our numberless transgressions in action, in word, in thought, in feeling, in desire, in purpose, and in inclination. This is set forth by the lamb being "roast with fire!"

With unleavened bread they should eat it. We have been reading in the 1st Epistle to the Corinthians what is set forth by the unleavened bread. There leaven, as leaven, signifies malice and wickedness; but the unleavened bread signifies sincerity and truth. And this is what we have particularly to aim at, that we are found in a state of uprightness! Uprightness is brought before us by this unleavened bread. The very opposite to guile, the very opposite to hypocrisy. Uprightness of heart, this is what God desires in His children! God bears with the weakness of His children, the infirmities of His children; but He does not bear with hypocrisy, with guile, with insincerity. He wants us to be upright, sincere, and without guile; and therefore we have to ask God continually that, in the riches of His grace, He would give unto us real, true, spiritual sincerity and uprightness and truth-that is, if really and truly we care about the revelation that He has been pleased to make in the Holy Scriptures, and seek to act according to the Word of God. A deeply important point this is-that we do not go our own way; that we do not seek to please ourselves; that we do not think we may do this, that, or the other thing, for God will not be particular. God will be particular! He cares about the Truth which He has put into our hands in the Holy Scriptures!

Then not merely was the lamb to be roast with fire and eaten with unleaven bread, but "with bitter herbs" they were to eat it. With bitter herbs. What might these be? I judge the herbs to be the deep consciousness the poor sinner has of his former life and deportment. We have forgiveness when we trust in the Lord Jesus Christ; all our numberless sins are forgiven! But though God has forgiven us, we cannot, so to speak, forgive ourselves; we continually remember all the ungodly life, and the ungodly ways, in which we went before our conversion. It is now seventy-two years and six weeks that I have been a believer in the Lord Jesus Christ, and for these seventy-two years I have known that everyone of my numberless transgressions is forgiven, and that not one of my numberless transgressions, in my unconverted days, shall be brought against me. But while I know that God has forgiven me perfectly, I cannot forgive myself! Day by day, more or less, my ungodly ways before I was converted, and all my numberless failings and shortcomings since my conversion, I remember against myself! These are "the bitter herbs" which I have while I am feeding on Christ! God has forgiven us; but we cannot, so to speak, forgive ourselves. We continually remember all our former ungodliness.

"Eat not of it raw, nor sodden at all with water, but roast with fire; his head with his legs, and with the purtenance thereof." The purtenance being the heart, the lungs, the kidneys. All must be roasted, and the whole lamb was to be brought on the table. And around the whole lamb they were to gather; not around a roasted leg, or a shoulder, but round the whole lamb. Now, there is a meaning in this, and the meaning of it is that we have the whole Christ, with all His offices, with all the virtues of His blessing, and the benefits to be had from Him. He is our Teacher; He is our Guide; He is our Comforter; He is our Helper; He is our Strength; He is our Redeemer; He is our Brother; He is our Friend; He is our Bridegroom; He is our Husband. The believer has Christ in all His offices.

This is set forth by the Israelites gathering round the whole lamb; not a piece cut up. But there is more than what I have said in this. It is this, that we have not to think we have to do with a part of the Saviour, or a part of the blessing of the Saviour; but that just as we need, poor, feeble, worthless worms as we are, whatever we require for our soul, it is to be found in the Lord Jesus Christ. And we never need in spiritual things to despair because our necessities are so great! However great our spiritual necessities are, all, all that we require is to be obtained through faith in the Lord Jesus Christ; through feeding on the Lord Jesus, through eating spiritually His flesh, and drinking spiritually His blood. All this is set forth by the fact that the Israelites were to gather round the whole lamb.

There is another point of great instruction. The believers in the Lord Jesus Christ, and believers in Him alone, are those who should be baptised. "Believer's baptism," therefore, is the right ordinance, and the only right ordinance, regarding baptism. It is not a question how old we are; but the question is, that we are believers in the Lord Jesus Christ when baptised. Now, while this is the right attention to the ordinance, we have to guard against this, that we do not assemble together as "baptised believers;" but that we assemble together as believers in the Lord Jesus Christ. It is not a part of the Truth of God round about which we have to meet, but round about Jesus we have to meet. That is the point. That is the set point. All believers must gather round the Whole Lamb! It is not this part of truth, or another part of truth. For instance, the truth of God is that the Lord Jesus Christ will come again before the Millennium, and will not come again after the Millennium has commenced; but He will come to introduce the Millennium, and there will be no Millennium without the Lord Jesus Christ; so that the Lord Jesus Christ in person is coming again! This is the truth of God, and which on no account we have to give up. But while this is so deeply important a truth, we should not meet together as those who hold this truth, but we should meet together as believers in Christ. We should meet together as those who trust in the Atoning Death of the Lord Jesus Christ! It is round about Christ we should meet! These are the points that are set forth in the fact that the whole lamb was to be gathered round about.

"Eat not of it raw, nor sodden at all with water, but roast with fire." And the head was not to be cut off previously. "His head with his legs." They were not to be cut off, but all roasted, and then brought on the table. "And with the purtenance thereof." "And ye shall let nothing of it remain until the morning: and that which remaineth of it until the morning, ye shall burn with fire; and thus shall ye eat it, with your loins girded, your shoes on your feet, and your staff in your hand, and ye shall eat it in haste: it is the Lord's Passover." Here the statement brings plainly before us the way in which persons are to be dressed and attired when going on a journey. The large loose gown was to be girded to the loins, that the traveller's marching or walking might not be retarded. Then, his shoes on! Because there might be a rough road; all kinds of things might be in the way, thorns, sharp stones, which would hurt the feet; therefore they were to put on their shoes! Then, the staff in the hand: another thing that is found in the traveller.

Now, this brings before us the deeply important truth that the moment we become believers in Christ, or for the first time feed on Christ, our own Passover Lamb, from that moment we become strangers and pilgrims in the world; we belong no longer to the world, for this world abides with the wicked one, is in intimate connection with the devil, and with the powers of darkness. From it, therefore, we are separated the moment we belong to Christ, and feed for the first time on the Lord Jesus Christ. Then we become strangers on earth; we set out on the journey, and this journey is heavenward. The end of the journey will be heaven! O how precious is this! My beloved brethren and sisters in Christ, do you all enter into this, that heaven is your home. I have, for seventy-two years, looked at it in that way, and it has made me a very happy man. Trials and difficulties, sorrows and afflictions, and disappointments I have had a great many of; I might say I have had them by hundreds, if not nearly by thousands, but, notwithstanding all, I have been during the seventy-two years and the six weeks I have now been a believer in Christ an exceedingly happy man, because I have always looked to the end of the journey. I am as certain that I shall be in heaven as if I were there already; not a shadow of a doubt about it, and I have never had a shadow of a doubt about it during the last seventy-two years.

And this is what, my beloved brethren and sisters, you should seek more and more to aim at, if you have not already attained to it; though I have no doubt that very many, if not most of you, have done so. But if there is anyone here who has not yet attained to it that heaven is their home, let them cry mightily to God that they may be sure of it, that heaven is their home. Now, I walk up and down in my room, and say to myself I am a sinner, a great sinner, and deserve nothing but punishment, but I shall not be punished, because my precious Lord Jesus was punished in my stead, and because I put my trust in Him. Therefore, nothing remains to me but heaven, and every day brings me a day nearer to it. See how precious is this. That is what we should feed on continually, and ponder continually. Consider what the Lord Jesus has done in our room and stead, and that salvation is completed by Him, and He will see to it that you and I, as assuredly as we are believers, shall be in heaven. And all this is perceived, and is set forth, in this verse. It is the person who believes in Christ setting out on a journey. He may have long to travel; but the end is what he has to look at. The end; and the end will be glory, the end will be heaven! We, poor miserable sinners, deserve nothing but punishment, but if we put our trust in the Lord Jesus the end of the journey will be glory, will be heaven! And we shall be for Eternity with the Lord JESUS Christ! O how precious this is; and I, by the grace of God, have been enabled for these seventy-two years to look at it in that way, and it has made me for all these years a very happy man!

The 12th verse, "For I will pass through the land of Egypt this night, and will smite all the firstborn in the land of Egypt, both men and beast."

Let us ponder-the firstborn of the king, the firstborn of the poor. "And against all the gods of Egypt I will execute judgment: I am the Lord." The judges, the princes, and the great ones of the earth, who are said to be the representatives of God here on earth, they shall be slain. Not merely the poor, but the lords therein, and every one of the kings, the princes, the judges, the great ones of the land.

Now the last verse, and a remarkable one it is; and we should seek particularly to ponder it. "And the blood shall be to you for a token upon the houses where ye are, and when I see the blood I will pass over you, and the plague shall not be upon you, to destroy you, when I smite the land of Egypt." Here we see what brought salvation, deliverance, safety to the Israelite! It was the blood of the Passover Lamb, which had been put on the door posts! Now, thus our salvation depends not upon our almsdeeds, not on church or chapel-going, not on what we have given, or intend to give, to the poor; on none of these things depend the salvation of the soul, but simply, solely, entirely, only, on the blood of the Lord Jesus Christ, which was shed for the remission of our sins, if we trust in it, depend upon it, look to it, and to it alone, for the salvation of our souls. That is the first point that we gather from this last verse. But there IS something else. "The blood shall be to you for a token on your houses where ye are, and when I see the blood I will pass over you, and the plague shall not come nigh to you." The eye of man might not be able to see the blood, but God saw the blood; the people inside the house might not be able to see it, the people outside the house might not be able to see it, but God saw it!

And now that brings before us that there may be among you, dear, true children of God, nervous ones, and very often, as a believer in Christ, I have clearly pointed out to them, for such and such reasons, they are truly believers in Christ, yet these nervous persons may not be able to see it! Now, must they go to hell because they cannot see it clearly regarding themselves? No! No! God, your Heavenly Father, He sees that, after all, you are really, truly, sincerely, alone looking to the blood of Jesus Christ; but on account of your nervous state you never come to the assurance you ought to, that you are saved; and for your comfort, I say that just as God in the dark night saw the blood, so God sees now, though these sincere, honest, upright, dear children of God, on account of their nervousness, do not see it.

Now, in conclusion, "Are we all convinced that we are sinners needing a Saviour?" Let us ask ourselves, young and old, male and female, aged and young, "Do I see that I am a sinner?" If not, O ask God to show it to you. No one can get to heaven without seeing that he is a sinner. All the people who go to hell have only a good opinion about themselves, and see nothing at all of their sinnership! You must come to see that you are a sinner-you must come to it, and see that you deserve punishment; and if you have not yet come to it, you won't get to heaven without it! Therefore, ask God to show you clearly that you are a sinner, that you are a sinner needing a Saviour. And what will you come to when you see it? You will seek to live a better life, but to make up for your past misconduct you will never be able to do. Never! Never! There is but One Who can make up for our transgressions; that is Jesus, Who yielded His perfect obedience to God, His own life, Who suffered the punishment which we deserve on account of our numberless transgressions. And if we trust in Him, and depend on Him for salvation, that is enough.

Therefore, the next point is to believe in Christ. That means to trust in Him for salvation, and if you say "I wish I could do that, but I am not able to do it," and you are sincerely wishing to put your trust in Him, He will show you, He will help you. But, remember, when we have come to it that we see we are sinners, we are to put our trust in Christ! One point more, and that is, that we seek for the whole remainder of our life to live to the praise, and honour, and glory of our Saviour, and that we ask Him day by day to aid us! May He bless us for His Name's sake. Amen.

Chapter 11: "The God of all grace . . . make you perfect, stablish . . . you."

A Sermon preached at Bethesda Chapel, Great George Street, Bristol, on Sunday Evening, March 28th, 1897·

1 Peter 5:10.

IN MEDITATING FOR a little while on this verse, let us notice, in the first place, the title given to our precious Heavenly Father. He is called "The God of all Grace!" He is God Almighty. He is the God of Power, the God of Justice, the God of Holiness, the God of Wisdom, the God of Infinite Compassion. He bears a variety of precious names, because they set forth His attributes, and prove, all of them, His character.

Now, in this portion He is called "The God of all Grace." That is a most precious title given to Him for our comfort. We are sinners, we fail in a variety of ways, we have failed in numberless ways before this; and we therefore need One Who is not merely Almighty, not merely righteous, not merely infinitely holy, not merely infinitely wise, but Who is also full of pity and compassion towards poor sinners, such as I am, and as you are. And therefore this word, that "He is the God of all Grace," suits us admirably. We just need such a God as this is. "He is the God of all grace," and were He not, O what would become of us? But because "He is the God of all grace" there is hope for the oldest, the greatest, the vilest sinner among us. None need to despair, since "He is the God of all Grace." That is, the grace that is found in God is without limit, and it can be applied to every one of our various failures and shortcomings, of whatever character they may be.

There is even the possibility that the greatest thief, the greatest robber, the vilest person that ever lived under heaven, can obtain forgiveness for his crimes. There is grace found in God, since "He is the God of all Grace," that whatever amount of grace is needed, it is to be had from Him. It is to be found in God. The greatest sins can be forgiven. Look at Manasseh's case, and see what God did for him. He was swimming, as it were, in the blood of the individuals whom he had murdered; and his idolatry went beyond everything that had ever been seen. But after he was taken a prisoner, and he humbled himself before God-really and truly humbled himself before God-see how merciful and good God was to him. It was all forgiven! There is an instance of "the God of all Grace!"

Look, again, at the great persecutor Saul, who delighted in having the believers in Christ beaten in every synagogue; who delighted in having them cast into prison, again and again and again; who delighted in tormenting them till they blasphemed the worthy, precious name of the Lord Jesus; who delighted in having believers in Christ put to death. Yet this great persecutor-in his day, we have reason to .believe, the greatest of persecutors-was forgiven. "I obtained mercy," he himself says. "I obtained mercy." Why? Because God was "the God of all Grace." That was the reason, not because he deserved it, not because he had become a better man now. No! While he was on the very way to Damascus, to do to the believers in Christ there what he had been doing to the believers in Jerusalem, the Lord Jesus met him and changed his heart, and made him one of the holiest men that ever lived on earth (as a mere human being, I mean) and this because God is "the God of all Grace." How this suits sinners, as we are, in all our variety of failures and shortcomings-even in the case of the converted. Though they hate sin and love holiness, yet how many are their failures, how many their shortcomings, how many their words which are contrary to the mind of God! Though they do not live in sin, and though they do not go on in an evil, wicked course, yet their failures, their shortcomings, if not in action, yet in word, and if it were even not in word, in thought, in feeling, in desire, in purpose, in inclination, O how many are they! How many are our failures and shortcomings! But our Friend and Helper in heaven, our Father in Christ Jesus, is "the God of all Grace."

O, a precious title! And I advise my beloved Christian friends to study this title yet further and further; to think about it, and to pray over this name given here to our Heavenly Father, that more and more they may be comforted by "the God of Grace," Who hath called us unto His eternal glory." That is the prospect we have! The weakest, the feeblest, the least instructed of the children of God have this prospect before them-to share the eternal glory of God! What a wonderful thing is this! And all the glory which the Father will give to the Lord Jesus Christ, on account of His mediatorial work, the weakest, the feeblest of the children of God shall share with Christ, because they are members of His mystical body, of which He is the Head, because they belong to Him; and that is the reason why they shall share it with Him. To this eternal glory of God the Father, and to this eternal glory of God the Son, we are called, and we have obtained (for the very purpose that we might be assured that we shall share it) an earnest, which is the Spirit of God. And as assuredly as we are the partakers of God the Holy Spirit, so surely we shall share the eternal glory of the Father and of the Son. Bright, and blessed, and glorious, therefore, are our prospects!

And how do we come to all this? What is our title to all this? It is stated, "Who hath called us unto His eternal glory by Christ Jesus"-rather in Christ Jesus, because we belong to Christ. No goodness, no merit, no worthiness found in us; not because we are better than other people; not because we pray a great deal; not because we work a great deal for God. That is not the reason, but because we are in Christ Jesus, members of His mystical body. The righteousness of Christ is imputed to us. He, in our room and stead, fulfilled the whole law, the law which we had broken times without number. And thus it comes that we are justified before God-that is, accounted just, reckoned just, though unjust and unrighteous in ourselves.

This perfect obedience of the Lord Jesus Christ unto death, the death on the Cross, is put to our account, is imputed to us; and therefore it is that we are called unto His eternal glory through Christ Jesus. The Lord Jesus Christ suffered in our room and stead, as our mediator, and bore all the punishment which we deserve on account of our numberless transgressions. And thus God, though just and holy and righteous, can in Christ Jesus give to us this wonderful blessing, to share His own eternal glory, and to share the eternal glory of the Lord Jesus Christ! O the wonderful, wondrous prospects which we have! If this were entered into, we should sing and rejoice all the day long, under all circumstances, under all trials; but because we enter so little into it, we apprehend so little of it, we pass by so much of what is declared in the Word of God about these things, and are so short of happiness as we are! Now let us ponder more abundantly all these things, that the heart may be brimful of joy. This is so important, because "the joy of the Lord" is the spiritual strength of the believer while we are this side eternity.

"Called us unto His eternal glory in Christ Jesus, after that ye have suffered awhile"-more exactly and minutely, "after ye have suffered a little while." It is only a little while, in comparison with eternity! Suppose it were to last 20 years, or 50 years, or even 80 years, and if it were even longer than this, yet, in comparison with eternity, it is a little while! For a little while only! O how short it will be, in comparison with eternity! We must never lose sight of the fact that eternity is a period without end. A thousand years are as one day! A thousand years, a little time, a very little time! And ten hundred millions of years, a little time. Eternity only beginning, though a thousand millions of years shall have passed away! Only the beginning of eternity! And 50 millions, and 5,000 millions of years, O how little, how little a period in comparison with eternity.

So after this life, suffered a little while, what comes? He will "make you perfect, stablish, strengthen, settle you." It is a positive statement! It is not merely a wish, not merely a desire, on the part of the apostle, nor merely a prayer. But He will make you perfect! When you look at your spiritual conflicts now, remember they will not always remain. We shall have the victory, completely, through our Lord Jesus Christ. No temptations any longer! Nor hesitation whether we shall do a thing, or not do it-all this completely done away. The will of God will be declared to us, and instantaneously, without a second's hesitation, without a moment of pondering whether we shall do it or not, the heart will say, "Thy will, Heavenly Father, is my perfect delight; I shall rejoice in glorifying Thee, by doing what Thou wilt have me to do." This is the state of things to which we are hastening on! Perfect conformity to the mind of Christ! Perfect; universal, and eternal obedience to our Heavenly Father! When, hereafter in the glory, His holy pleasure is made known to us, instantaneously we shall comply. That is the meaning of being made perfect, and that is the promise we have.

He will make you perfect as to holiness and as to intelligence; there will be no remaining in ignorance found in us, but "we shall know in that day, as perfectly as we are known now." We shall completely know God, we shall completely know the Lord Jesus, we shall completely know everything that is according to the mind of God, or contrary to the mind of God. O the bright and blessed and glorious prospect that every particle of ignorance now found in us will be completely done away with. We shall be perfect as to holiness; we shall be perfect as to knowledge. O how bright, how glorious, these prospects are! We are not perfect now, even as to knowledge, or as to grace. Far otherwise. We are weak and feeble in ourselves still, though believers in the Lord Jesus; and though hating sin and loving holiness, we are far from being perfect. But we shall be perfect! This is the bright and blessed prospect, "He will make you perfect, stablish, strengthen, settle you."

Stablish-that is, He will give unto us a state in which there will no double-mindedness, all a reality, in regard to the things of God; all one-minded, all according to the mind of God. This is the bright prospect before us. Then we shall be strengthened -that is to say, completely firm according to the mind of God, no double-mindedness whatever; one mind, and only one mind, to glorify God; one purpose, and only one purpose, to live for God, to labour for God; and everything that is contrary to the mind of God will be entirely removed from us. A bright and blessed prospect this, that just as the Lord Jesus Christ was, while on earth, thirty-three years and a half, so hereafter will be the feeblest, the weakest, of the children of God; so completely minded shall we be, as the Lord Jesus Christ was, for glorifying God while on earth. That is the prospect before us.

And lastly, we shall be settled-that is, such a foundation of complete spirituality shall we be brought to, that a shaking of the foundation will be entirely impossible, O this prospect of being settled, with firm foundations, will be ours; no shifting and changing will be the question then, but one purpose, and one purpose throughout eternity, will be ours: to glorify God, to do the will of God, to work for God, to have no will of our own. O how bright is the prospect for us weak ones, feeble ones, and erring ones, as we are, that we shall not remain thus. O how often have we condemned ourselves since our conversion, in that we are not altogether Christ-like, that we are still not always inclined to do the things which are perfectly according to the mind of God, and though at last we come to it, and do the thing according; to the mind of God, yet that we hesitated for a little moment, that we considered whether we should do the thing or not. This should not be found in us; this shows that we are not altogether according to the mind of God, that yet the corrupt nature is found in us, that the devil has still a measure of power over us, and that we are not yet perfect in holiness.

All this will then be altered completely. One single aim throughout eternity, one single mind throughout eternity, to live for God, to glorify God, without the least particle of hesitation at any time; instantaneously, when the will of God is presented to us to set our seal to it, that we will obey Him, that we will glorify Him, that we will do His will. How bright and blessed and glorious these prospects! Now is there yet an unbeliever here present? If so, to you, my dear friend, I would say in whatever way you seek after happiness now, you will never have it, can never have it, except you find it in this way that I have been pointing out, I through Jesus Christ. The Apostles, holy men, exceedingly holy men as they were, obtained all this through Christ. They did not obtain it by their own exertion. It was as poor, guilty, hell-deserving sinners, they accepted what God gives to the sinner in Christ Jesus.

We have to own before God that we are sinners, and, if we do not see it, to ask God to show it to us, and then to confess before God in prayer that we are sinners, and, having done so, to put our trust solely in Christ Jesus for salvation. It is this, and this alone, which brings the blessing, and can bring the blessing. Any, therefore, who are not yet believers in Christ, if they desire really and truly to be happy, this is the only way to obtain it; if they desire to go to heaven, this is the only way to get there. God grant that some soul or other may be benefited through this our meditation, for Jesus Christ's sake. Amen.

Chapter 12: "Trust in the Lord."

A Sermon preached at Bethesda Chapel, Great George Street, Bristol, on Sunday Evening, May 30th, 1897

Proverbs 3:5-17.

THE BOOK OF Proverbs forms a deeply important portion of the Word of God. It is full of most precious counsels and advice for all human beings, if they would only give ear. Of course, believers in the Lord Jesus Christ will have the greatest blessing through it; but even for those who as yet do not know the Lord, if they were to attend to what is given in this Book of Proverbs, they would find great blessing and benefit, not merely in regard to the life to come, but for their stay here on earth. It is full of important instruction. I will mention just this point, for instance. More than once warning is given against becoming surety for other persons. Now, very many of us know, from our own experience, what misery, what exceeding great misery, has come upon whole families, it may be upon several families, simply on account of not attending to this.

Hastily, inconsiderately, they have become sureties for others, saying to themselves, "I shall never be called on to pay this money;" but before they were aware of it they were compelled to make good their suretyship, and often and often brought the greatest misery not merely on themselves, but on their whole family, and perhaps more than one family were drawn thus into misery. Now, God, knowing all this beforehand, through His servant Solomon admonished us not to do it. I myself, in my long life, have known instance upon instance of the greatest misery brought on whole families on account of not attending to this. Now, this is just one instance that I mention; but there are numberless points in the Book of Proverbs of a similar character, which, because they are not attended to, bring wretchedness and misery, not merely on one, but often on very many. Verse 5: " Trust in the Lord with all thine heart, and lean not unto thine own understanding." Often and often because this likewise has not been attended to misery has been brought, the greatest misery, not only on individuals, but on large families. The temptation is, "O I have a great deal of experience in my business; I know what to do, I know how to act, I know what will turn out best." Thus speculation has come on, and speculation to a very, very large extent; and misery beyond description has been brought about on account of this. I just mention one instance which I was intimate with, the individual concerned being one whom I greatly loved. There was a war with China coming on, many, many years ago-the first war with

China on the part of England; the individual was advised to buy an immense quantity of tea, because tea would rise in price exceedingly on account of the war, and the beloved, dear Christian man said to himself, "I do not care about this speculation for myself, but I feel exceedingly for my own dear brother about business matters." And so, being advised by the brother to buy an immense quantity, he speculated far beyond his capital, in order to help his brother out of difficulties. The result was, very soon war was at an end, the tea did not at all rise to what it was expected it would-indeed, because so many had bought very large quantities, it actually decreased in price, instead of rising-and this beloved Christian friend of mine lost an enormous sum of money, so that instead of helping his brother he brought himself into exceeding great difficulty.

Now here, you see, is the Word speaking to the opposite effect, "Trust in the Lord with all thine heart"-"depend on Me for what you need; look to Me for what you need, and do not take the advice of those brokers, or any other such agents, but consult the Lord"-"lean not unto thine own understanding." Do not suppose because you have had a good deal of experience, or another person has had a good deal of experience, that that is all which is needed; but betake yourself to the Lord under all circumstances, at all times, under all difficulties, and seek His advice and counsel. Now this has been my habit (it was not my habit for the first two years after my conversion), but it has now been for 69 years my habit to act according to this, and the result is that all has been going on well with my affairs. I have never been allowed to bring myself into difficulties on account of such matters, because I have not trusted in my own experience, but have trusted in the Lord.

If difficulties arise with our service, when we meet in the morning we lay our case before God, tell Him in all simplicity our position, and ask His counsel and advice. And He does give unto us counsel and advice, and helps us out of difficulties and perplexing circumstances, though they are very frequent in our service-yea, there is rarely a day but something or ether turns up in which we need to be guided and directed by the Lord; and He helps us, He appears for us. I can advise this way of living and acting to all my beloved Christian friends, for the result of it is peace, peace, peace! All the ordinary troubles of life vanish, if we thus throw our burden on the Lord and speak to Him about matters.

"Lean not unto thine own understanding." How dearly expressed, how decidedly expressed! Our danger is continually to lean on our own understanding; to say to ourselves, "O, I have many times passed through similar circumstances. I have a good deal of experience in these matters; it is not necessary that I should pray about it, for I know very well what I ought to do." And thus we bring on ourselves wretchedness and misery, and often not merely on ourselves, but on those connected with us.

"In all thy ways acknowledge Him, and He shall direct thy paths." In all thy ways. Let us particularly notice this-not merely now and then come to God for guidance and direction, but regarding every step that we take, every business that we enter into, and every new phase of our business, bring it before God and talk to Him, converse with Him concerning the matter. That is the meaning of "In all thy ways acknowledge Him;" and the result will be this: "He shall direct thy paths." Never begin anything without going to God about it in prayer! Never take any step without first of all settling the matter between yourselves and God, and the result will be you will not speak to Him in vain. He loves you. "He shall direct thy paths;" He will make plain your way, and show you clearly and distinctly how you ought to act. Thus you will escape the great difficulties, the great trials, in carrying out the measure of light which God will give you. O how precious!

Now, we have not to say, "I do not live in the days of miracles; I do not live in a time when there is a Urim and a Thummim, and the high priest who could tell me what to do." For God is willing by His Spirit, through the Holy Scriptures, yet in our day, at the close of the nineteenth century, to guide and direct us. And in being guided and directed, if we carry out the measure of light which God is pleased to give to us, we shall find how blessed it is not to take any steps directed by our own understanding, but to seek wisdom from God, and obtain counsel and advice from Him. The Lord Jesus Christ, among all other titles given to Him in the Word of God, has one title: that is, He is the Counsellor. The Counsellor of the Church of God, for her benefit, for her instruction. We are naturally ignorant, we do not know how to act, what to do; but if we betake ourselves to our Counsellor, the Lord Jesus Christ, we shall find how ready He is to counsel us, to advise us.

I have found it thus, more or less, during the last 69 years that I have known the Lord. The first two years I often, often acted hastily, without much prayer, because patience was not natural to me then. I would have the matter settled, and therefore acted without patiently and quietly waiting on God; and taking hasty steps often and often, I was not merely confounded, but I brought trouble on myself. During the last 69 years, however, I have acted differently, and have therefore gone peacefully along, and have had rest in God. None of those trials through which I first passed after my conversion have been found in my life since, because I have patiently and quietly waited on God, to guide, direct, and help me.

"Be not wise in thine own eyes; fear the Lord, and depart from evil." Naturally we have, often and often, too high an idea about ourselves; we are "wise in our own eyes," and on account of this take steps to go forward without seeking the counsel and advice of the Lord. The result is, trouble and difficulty. Now, beloved Christian friends, let us especially be warned by this, not to be wise in our own eyes, because it is too true, that we are not wise. If left to ourselves, we shall surely take wrong steps; we shall surely be confounded. Things will not go on well. And therefore it becomes us as being made fully aware of our natural ignorance and helplessness, to betake ourselves to God for counsel and advice. That is what we have to do, and above all to "fear God and to depart from evil."

Our own ways are so frequently connected with that which is contrary to the mind of God; but if we are not wise in our own eyes, not only shall we be guided aright, but the result, further, will be that taking steps according to the mind of God we shall be departing from evil. Now, what follows from this? It tends even to the benefit of the body. Not merely gives peace of mind to the soul, but is good even for the body. "It shall be health to thy navel and marrow to thy bones."

Now comes in another subject altogether. "Honour the Lord with thy substance, and with the first-fruits of all thy increase, so shall thy barns be filled with plenty, and thy presses shall burst out with new wine." I do not forget that the Israelites had special promises given to them with regard to abundance in this life, if they walked in the ways of the Lord. Now, though in this present dispensation, we have not the promise to become very rich, to become great men, if we walk in the ways of the Lord, still there is, if we attend to these two verses, blessing coming to us even in this life, besides spiritual blessing. I have known this in my own experience, by acting according to these two verses. I have seen it ever so many times in the lives of godly brethren and sisters in Christ, who acted according to these two verses.

"Honour the Lord with thy substance and with the first-fruits of all thy increase." God fills the clouds with rain, for the very purpose that they may empty themselves on the land, to make the land fertile; and so God trusts His children, as His stewards, with means not to keep all to themselves, not to enjoy merely themselves, but to communicate out of the abundance He is pleased to give them to their fellow men-those who are weak and feeble, and cannot work, or who through other circumstances are brought into straightened, difficult positions and circumstances. This attended to brings blessing not only to the soul, but even blessing of a temporal character. I speak as one who knows all this from an experience in my own case of much more than 60 years. I speak about this as having, through my acquaintance with more than tens of thousands of children of God, had brought before me again and again and again the fact that those who acted according to the principles here laid down, not merely brought blessings to their souls, but even as to their circumstances temporarily, obtained far more again than they had given away, so that not only interest was given them, but compound interest, and in many cases twenty times, fifty times, even a hundred times more than they had given to the poor, or than they had given to the work of God. For God ever sees to it that He is not our debtor, but that we are His debtors. O if brethren and sisters in Christ habitually acted according to this verse, how different would be their position even as to this life, and how great the blessing which they would thus bring to their own souls!

"Honour the Lord with thy substance." When God is pleased to give to us temporal blessings, He gives them, not that on our own persons we may spend the abundance He is pleased to bestow on us, but that we may remember the weak and sickly, and help and assist them; that we may remember those who are out of employment, who would gladly work, but who have no work; and that we may care for the widow, and the aged widow in particular, and the aged man who can no longer work-that we may remember their necessities and care for them. And the result will be, as I have seen it times without number in my long Christian career, that not only will blessing come to the souls of those who act according to this word, but that even with regard to temporal things God will abundantly repay what we have thus given. "So shall thy barns be filled with plenty, and thy presses shall burst out with new wine." We may have no barns, and no vineyard, to have this literally fulfilled; but God, in some way or other, will make it manifest how He is mindful of what we have given to the widow, to the poor sick person who cannot work, to the poor aged man who is past work.

Now comes another subject. "My son, despise not the chastening of the Lord; neither be weary of His correction, for whom the Lord loveth He correcteth, even as a father the son in whom he delighteth." Often and often I have found how real, true children of God are discouraged, disheartened, greatly bowed down, because they are so long afflicted, forgetting that the very affliction is a token of the Father's love to them. O remember this, because it is a matter not to question. I take God at His word, "Whom the Lord loveth He correcteth." All these afflictions are education to our hearts. In regard to our positions and circumstances, "Whom the Lord loveth He correcteth, even as a father the son in whom he delighteth;" not the father the son whom he hates, whom he does not care about in the least, whom he despises, whom he may mean to disinherit. Nothing, nothing, nothing of the kind. "Even as a father the son in whom he delighteth." Ah! if this were laid to heart by the dear children of God in trial, in affliction, and in difficulty, how differently would they judge their trials, their afflictions, their disappointments, their sorrows, their pain and suffering. "My son, despise not the chastening of the Lord."

I was once for a good while in a position that I could not work at all, because I had overwrought myself, overworked myself in service for the Lord, had not been careful at all about my health. For six years, I had never taken a walk in the fields! If the work of the Lord called me to exercise, I would walk eight, ten, twenty miles, or more in such service, but if the work of the Lord did not call me to exercise, I would never go out for five minutes for the sake of recreation, or for the sake of benefiting my health. The consequence was, that while before I was able to write ten, fifteen, or twenty letters without rising from my chair, and read for three or four hours at a stretch, I was now so reduced that the writing of one single little note was too much for me, and, as for reading, not a quarter of an hour could I stay at it. It was all too much. Under these circumstances I did not, by the grace of God, despise His chastening; but, after months and months had passed, leaving me in this state, I began to be weary of His correction. That was the danger into which I came, and I began to ask God not merely to keep me from despising the chastening, but not to weary-to be willing to go on bearing with the way in which He dealt with me. And, in the riches of His grace, He kept me from being weary.

So after months had been passed in this weakness mentally, in the inability of going on doing what I had been able to do, my health became by little and little restored; and I thus obtained the ability of warning my fellow-believers to take care of their health. I began to take now and then a little rest, now and then a little walk; and the consequence was I have been able to work far, far more abundantly, and have been far, far happier in my soul since I began to care about my health. I mention this for warning to those who despise the taking care of their health, and go on toiling, toiling, toiling, as if their bodies were brass and iron. If we wish to get profit to the soul, we need to let the body have rest. I state deliberately and solemnly, in the fear of God, during these last fifty years of my life, since I have allowed myself a quarter of an hour's rest, or a little more, now and then, God has enabled me to labour far more abundantly than before, and my soul has also been blest far more abundantly.

"My son, despise not the chastening of the Lord; neither be weary of His correction." Let this sink into our souls-not to be weary of His correction. It does not require overmuch grace not to despise the chastening of the Lord; but it requires a good deal of grace when the mental affliction, the chastening of the Lord, continues for a long time, not to be weary of His correction. But the will of God is to submit to His dealings with us, and His leadings of us, both now and always; for "whom the Lord loveth He correcteth." This is a word for particular support under affliction, to remember that it is a love token when we are afflicted. "Whom the Lord loveth He correcteth, even as a father the son in whom he delighteth." Notice this phrase, "In whom he delighteth." Therefore it is entirely a mistake to suppose that when affliction, trial, or sorrow is allowed to befall us, that it is a token of dislike on the part of God; but it is all intended for blessing to our souls. Because God loves us, He gives us this love-token of affliction.

"Happy is the man that findeth wisdom, and the man that getteth understanding." Now, this is particularly a word to those who are not converted, for "finding wisdom" means to be brought to the fear of the Lord. Wisdom is the fear of the Lord, to know the Saviour, to see that we are sinners, to own that we are sinners, to confess that we are sinners; and then to put our trust in the Lord Jesus Christ for the salvation of our souls. That is the meaning of finding wisdom. Now, before going on any further, I affectionately ask the little company here present, " Are we all believers in the Lord Jesus Christ?" God's delight is to make us all as happy as we are capable of being while yet in the body. Now, have we obtained this real, true happiness, everyone of us, through faith in the Lord Jesus? That is my desire and my prayer regarding all here present.

There is nothing to hinder us individually from obtaining the blessing. I was as far from God as anyone possibly could be; but it pleased God to show me what a great sinner I was. I owned it before God, and He helped me to put my trust alone in Jesus for salvation; and thus I became a very happy young man, and am continuing to hold fast to Christ, to trust in Him alone for salvation, and, by grace, to walk in the fear of God. I have now been for more than 71 years a very happy man. And thus blessing is to be obtained by everyone, for God does not act by partiality, or despise this or another one; He takes delight and pleasure in bestowing this happiness on any and every one He has to do with.

But there are some individuals who will not have it, who are determined to go their own way, who despise the blessing which God is willing to give to them in Christ Jesus, and therefore they are without it, and they will remain without it as long as they continue in this state of mind. But let us not forget what is said here. "Happy is the man that findeth wisdom." That means, happy is the man who comes to Christ, happy is the man who puts his trust in the Lord Jesus Christ; and here those who have not yet done so will find it thus if they will close with Christ, if they will but own that they are sinners needing a Saviour. Then, having confessed this, having put their trust in the Lord Jesus Christ, God will account them just and righteous for Christ's sake, God will forgive them their sins for Christ's sake, and this will bring peace to the soul, rest to the soul, and make them happy through faith in Christ Jesus. "Happy is the man that findeth wisdom." I say once more, wisdom means the fear of God. "Findeth the fear of God; " and this is brought about through faith in Christ Thus we are regenerated, born again, get spiritual life and a new nature, by 'which we hate sin and love holiness. Though it be but little and little at the first, yet we shall increase more and more in this.

"And the man that getteth understanding"-that is, getteth understanding about heavenly things, about his own sinfulness; about God and the Lord Jesus Christ; and about the vanity of this present world and the blessedness of heavenly things. "For the merchandise of it is better than the merchandise of silver, and the gain thereof than fine gold; she is more precious than rubies, and all the things thou canst desire are not to be compared unto her." In this figurative language is brought before us the blessedness of being believers in Christ, the blessedness of having found wisdom, and of having obtained a new nature, spiritual life, justification, and the forgiveness of all our sins. "The merchandise of it is better than the merchandise of silver"-that is, whatever we might gain in the possession of silver, it is all as nothing in comparison with getting Christ. "And the gain thereof than fine gold." To have found Jesus is better, better by far, than an abundance of fine gold. "She is more precious than rubies." Wisdom, the fear of God obtained through faith in the Lord Jesus Christ, is more precious than rubies or pearls, "and all the things thou canst desire are not to be compared unto her." A very large property left to us, as a legacy, is nothing in comparison with finding Christ. A very lucrative situation is nothing in comparison with Christ. A very high post under Government is nothing in comparison with Christ. All the blessings of this present life, all is nothing in comparison with finding Jesus. O let this sink deeply into our hearts. "She is more precious than rubies." In other words, "Jesus is more precious than pearls, than rubies; and all the things thou canst desire are not to be compared unto Him."

"Length of days is in her right hand, and in her left hand riches and honour." This is particularly to be looked at in a spiritual point of view. The eternal life, eternal happiness, is our lot-is that which we obtain through faith in the Lord Jesus. "And in her left hand riches and honour." That is, spiritual riches and spiritual honours, because we become the inheritors of God and of the Lord Jesus; honours because we shall share with the Lord Jesus Christ the glory which the Father gives Him as a recompense for His mediatorial work as our Saviour. We shall have the honour with Him; He will not have it merely to Himself. His Bride, the Church of God, will share it with Him, and therefore shall we partake of the honour which the Father gives to Him.

"Her ways are ways of pleasantness, and all her paths are peace." I cannot tell you what a happy man I became when I found the Lord Jesus. I had been seeking year after year for happiness; but I met with nothing but disappointment and increased guilt on the conscience as long as I was not a believer in Christ. But when I found Jesus, I became a truly happy young man, and I have been a truly happy man now for 71 years and six months. I have had fulfilled in my own experiences what is stated here-that the ways of wisdom are the ways of pleasantness. Numberless persons think it is far from being pleasant to become a Christian; they think if they were to become believers in the Lord Jesus Christ they would not have a happy day more. This is the greatest folly, the greatest mistake, for our real true happiness commences only when we find the Lord Jesus Christ; therefore we need not to be pitied as believers in Christ, but others are to be counselled to seek the same Lord whom we have found, in order that they, too, may partake of the happiness which we have obtained through faith in Him.

Then, lastly, "All her paths are peace." Now, if at any time we are without peace, we should ask ourselves, "What is the reason? Am I really walking in the ways of wisdom, for it is stated that all her paths are peace? If I am without peace, it becomes me solemnly, earnestly, and carefully, to look into the matter, and see whether I have not departed from the ways of the Lord, whether I have not forsaken the fear of the Lord; for if I were going on in the paths of wisdom I should be at peace." O how instructive is all this!

Now, my beloved Christian friends, I have been directed, after a good deal of prayer, to the words on which we have been meditating, and I beseech and entreat you all to ponder again and again and again these verses, and to remember the remarks which I have made in connection with them; for weighty and important matters are contained in these verses, and, if attended to, the result will be happiness in a way in which as yet we have not known it. And, again, should there be any present who are not yet believers in the Lord Jesus Christ, they should give themselves no rest in asking God to show them that they are sinners, and that they need the Saviour; and when they are brought to know this, then to ask God to enable them to put their trust in Jesus. And what they will obtain will be the forgiveness of their sins and peace to their souls, and hatred of sin and love for holiness. God grant this blessing to all of us, for Christ's sake.

Chapter 13: "He was wounded for our transgressions."

A Sermon preached at Bethesda Chapel, Great George Street, Bristol, on April 25th, 1897

Isaiah 53.

THIS CHAPTER WAS written by the Holy Ghost, through the prophet Isaiah, 740 years before the birth of our Lord Jesus Christ; and all that we read here regarding Him was fulfilled in His life, and in His atoning work. Another most precious truth out of many thousands that the Word of God is its own proof. It is not at all necessary to have external evidences that the Holy Scriptures are the Word of God! They themselves are proof of its truths! The commencement of the chapter plainly indicates that multitudes might hear and read what is revealed by the Holy Ghost in this portion, and yet the message of God be not received. "Who hath believed our report?" Comparatively a small number! "To whom is the Arm of Jehovah revealed?" The Lord Jesus Christ is called here "the Arm of Jehovah." Even as our arm is the great instrument by which we work in connection with the body, so the Lord Jesus Christ was God's great Instrument in working; and therefore He is called " The Arm of Jehovah." "For He shall grow up before Him as a tender plant, and as a root out of a dry ground; He hath no form nor comeliness, and when we shall see Him, there is no beauty that we should desire Him." This brings before us, in figure, the outward meanness of the Lord Jesus Christ, and the inferiority of His position in the world.

In the first place, it is stated, "He shall grow up before Him as a tender plant." A tender plant, a very little plant; just something springing up out of a tree cut down-yet a little life in the root, and a little shooting forth. This refers to the Lord Jesus in being connected with the House of David, the Son of David. The might and power and wealth and riches, seen in the days of Solomon, were all done with; His mother, after the flesh, so poor that she was unable to bring a lamb for an offering, but must be content with a pair of turtle doves. Not merely a tender plant, but "a root out of a dry ground." Water is wanted to make it become larger and larger, for it is found only in a dry ground. "He hath no form nor comeliness." All the representations of the Lord Jesus Christ as an exceedingly beautiful man, all are fancy representations. Nothing of the kind, so far as His outward appearance was concerned. There was "no form nor comeliness" found in Him. "When we shall see Him, there is no beauty that we should desire Him," for it was on purpose that there should be no attraction according to the eye of the flesh.

"He is despised and rejected of men." This was His standing in the world. Instead of being honoured by everyone, sought after by everyone, it was the very opposite. "He was despised and rejected of men; a man of sorrows, and acquainted with grief." That was one reason why there was nothing attractive in His appearance, because of the sorrow that was continually found in Him, on account of the ungodliness in all directions surrounding Him. This filled His heart with grief; and therefore no comeliness was found in Him. "And we hid, as it were, our faces from Him," because of there being no attraction at all to nature. His very appearance was always indicating His communion with God; His perfect holiness; His abhorring that which was hateful to God. Therefore those who were not likeminded with Him "hid their faces from Him."

"He was despised, and we esteemed Him not; surely He hath borne our griefs, and carried our sorrows, yet we did esteem Him stricken, smitten of God, and afflicted." The great mass of the people regarded Him as suffering on account of His own sins; on account of that which was wrong in Him they considered Him "stricken, smitten of God, and afflicted." But the next two verses tell us the true reason. "But He was wounded for our transgressions, He was bruised for our iniquities; the chastisement of our peace was upon Him, and with His stripes we are healed. All we like sheep have gone astray; we have turned everyone to his own way, and the Lord hath laid on Him the iniquity of us all." On these two verses I say nothing now, because we shall more especially meditate on them presently.

"He was oppressed and He was afflicted, yet He opened not His mouth; He is brought as a lamb to the slaughter, and as a sheep before her shearers is dumb, so He opened not His mouth." The meekness, the gentleness, the patient suffering, the passing through heavy trials and afflictions without fretting or complaining, far less murmuring, is here brought before us. One of the figures used, "As a sheep," etc., is very remarkable. I have seen again and again, with my own eyes, when sheep are shorn, that instead of resisting and making a noise, they very patiently bear it. And thus is the word fulfilled. "As a sheep before her shearers is dumb, so He (the Lord Jesus Christ) opened not His mouth."

"He was taken from prison and from judgment; and who shall declare His generation? For He was cut off out of the land of the living; for the transgression of My people was He stricken." This refers to the resurrection of the Lord Jesus Christ-"He was taken from prison and from judgment." "Who shall declare His generation?" In consequence of what the Lord Jesus Christ did, and what He suffered, I here should be given Him a multitude of believers: this is the generation that cannot be counted. "He was cut off out of the land of the living;" and this was done not on account of His transgressions, but "For the transgression of My people was He stricken." In our room and stead He suffered, and as our substitute.

"And He made His grave with the wicked." That is, as if He had been an ordinary man, and especially as if He had been a wicked man. "And with the rich in His death." That refers particularly to the splendid grave He had, in being buried in the sepulchre of Joseph of Arimathea, a grave which was cut out of the rock, and therefore exceedingly costly. "Because He had done no violence." The word "because" here is rather more correctly in the Hebrew, "although." "Although He had done no violence, neither was any deceit in His mouth," yet had He to die, and to be buried, just as if He had been a sinner like ourselves.

"Yet it pleased the Lord to bruise Him." This bruising Him refers to the greatness of His agonies and sufferings in His atoning death. "He hath put Him to grief; when Thou shalt make His soul an offering for sin, He shall see His seed, He shall prolong His days, and the pleasure of the Lord shall prosper in His hand." All this is now being fulfilled. The soul of the Lord Jesus, or the life of the Lord Jesus, has been made an offering for sin. He does see His seed. O the numberless millions who have been brought to the knowledge of Jesus Christ since His crucifixion, and O the thousands upon thousands, and the tens of thousands upon tens of thousands, who are continually being brought to believe on Him. "He shall prolong His days." He is living now after His resurrection; though 1860 years and upwards have passed already, He is the Living One, and after thousands upon thousands of years shall have passed away, and millions upon millions of years have gone, He will still be the Living One. And thus the fulfilment of the Word, "He shall prolong His days."

But this is not all, for "The pleasure of the Lord shall prosper in His hand." The atoning work has been carried on these 1860 years, and will be carried on till all is completed, till Satan has been entirely confounded, and the works of the devil have been completely destroyed. Thus the atoning work has been going on, and thus the fulfilment of the prophecy, "The pleasure of Jehovah shall prosper in His hand." Satan has sought to resist it continually, but has been as frequently foiled, and the work of the Lord, in the midst of all the opposition of Satan, still goes on!

"He shall see of the travail of His soul, and shall be satisfied." There are not a few present this very evening who are regenerated by the power of the Holy Ghost, through faith in the Lord Jesus Christ. Thus the fulfilment, "He shall see of the travail of His soul, and shall be satisfied." And this very day we have reason to believe that multitudes, considering the whole number of human beings on earth to whom the Gospel has been proclaimed, have been brought to the knowledge of Jesus Christ; thereby further fulfilling this word. "By His knowledge shall My Righteous Servant justify many." "My Righteous Servant," that is a title given to the Lord Jesus Christ. By knowing Him, many shall be justified; that is, brought into a state, through faith, that Jehovah can count them just and righteous, though unjust and unrighteous in themselves. That is the meaning of being justified. "For He shall bear their iniquities." By reason of these individuals having a Substitute, Who in their room; fulfilled the law of God and Who in their room bore the punishment of the law, they are justified.

"Therefore will I divide Him a portion with the great, and He shall divide the spoil with the strong." Satan, the angels of Satan, the powers of darkness, these are the strong ones here referred to; but the Lord Jesus Christ gets the victory, takes the prey out of their hands, and therefore gets the glory to Himself. "Because He hath poured out His soul unto death, and He was numbered with the transgressors, and He bare the sin of many, and made intercession for the transgressors." This, again, has had its fulfilment, and is going on being fulfilled in our day, and will be fulfilled while the Lord Jesus Christ tarries.

Verses 5 and 6 bring especially before us the vicarious sufferings of our Lord Jesus Christ, that He, as our Substitute, not merely fulfilled the law of God, which we have broken times without number, but that He, likewise standing in our place, endured the punishment due to us, on account of our numberless transgressions. For this reason these two verses axe exceedingly precious, and are to be present in our hearts and our faith, in our life and deportment, and are continually to be looked at and applied to our life and conduct, in order that, in the midst of all our failures and shortcomings, as long as we do not wilfully go on in a course contrary to the mind of God, we may have "peace and joy in the Holy Ghost."

The very first word, how precious! "Surely." "Surely," it is said in the 4th verse, "He hath borne our griefs." "Surely" He hath "carried our sorrows, yet we did esteem Him stricken, smitten of God, and afflicted." But! O what a "but" this is! "But He was wounded for our transgressions." The whole in regard to the sufferings of Christ is to be put aside, and simply are we to look at it in reference to ourselves, as if we were the people, and the only people, for whom He endured all this. And it is just in the degree in which we are able to apply the atoning work of the Lord Jesus Christ to ourselves, and to enter into it with reference to themselves, that comfort, peace, and joy in the Holy Ghost results. If we think at all upon other persons, we do not to the full degree, as otherwise we might, obtain the blessing. We should write, as it were, our own name on the fifth verse, and say to ourselves, individually, as believers. "He was wounded for my transgressions. He was bruised for my iniquities; the chastisement of my peace was upon Him "-that is, that I might have peace in my soul and be at peace with God, therefore He had to suffer-"and with His stripes I am healed." And thus applying the whole to ourselves, the result will be the heart will be brimful of peace and joy in the Holy Ghost; while, on the other hand, the more we look at the sufferings of Christ, the atonement He made, with reference to others, the less will peace and joy in the Holy Ghost result from it. "He was wounded for our transgressions." Here we have especially not to lose sight of the fact that it was not merely bodily pain and suffering which our Lord Jesus had to endure-though, unquestionably, that was exceedingly great-but He passed through "the hour of darkness," and His holy, righteous soul had to suffer. And in connection with all this, we have never to lose sight of the fact that the Father did not deliver at that time, in order that, really and truly, He might pass through all the woe, the misery, the agonies, and pain, and suffering of body, mind, and spirit through which we ought to have passed, on account of our numberless transgressions. All this we have to carefully consider, in order to get the least idea of the greatness of the sufferings through which our blessed Lord had to pass.

Then it is further stated, "He was bruised for our iniquities." Ground, as it were, in the mill to powder by His sufferings-something like this is brought before us by the expression, "Bruised for our iniquities." O the vastness of the sufferings, the greatness of the agonies, through which our Lord had to pass! And O how this should make us to abhor ourselves on account of sin, for our sins brought all this on our Lord. Speaking after the manner of men, had we been free of sin, had all human beings been perfectly free from sin, the atonement would not have been necessary! But by the fall, sin being introduced into the world and all human beings to a greater or less degree being actually transgressors, and guilty of sinful deeds, sinful, unholy words, sinful, unholy thoughts, desires, purposes, and inclinations, therefore, in order that we might be reconciled to God, that we might be cleansed from all our numberless transgressions, the Lord Jesus Christ had to endure all this, so that we could be saved finally. "He was bruised for our iniquities." I ask, affectionately, my beloved brethren and sisters in Christ, to ponder this word, "bruised."

"The chastisement of our peace was upon Him." That is, He was chastised in order that we might have peace in our souls, and in order that we might be reconciled unto God. He had to endure all that which we ourselves ought to have endured; but if we put our trust in Him, if we look at the atonement of the Lord Jesus Christ with regard to ourselves, then we shall have peace in our souls, and be at peace with God, because what the Lord Jesus Christ endured, He endured vicariously, on account of our numberless transgressions. "And with His stripes we are healed." The moment we believe in the Lord Jesus Christ, we obtain the Lord Jesus Christ as a Spiritual Physician, and get under His care, and are placed in a kind of spiritual hospital; and there we remain, under the care of this infinitely great Physician, who watches over us, who looks after us, and who does not discharge us as incurable ones, as many people are discharged from the hospitals in the world. Not thus! Not thus! But "The Great Physician" remains through the whole life we spend on earth "Our Great Physician," and we remain under His care and keeping temporally and · spiritually. In His own great, precious spiritual hospital, we are kept till we are perfectly cured, perfectly healed. The moment we believe in

Jesus Christ, He becomes our Physician. The moment we believe in the Lord Jesus Christ we are placed under His care, for being perfectly healed. And the same moment we are entered in the hospital of the Lord Jesus, and there kept and looked after, and attended to by the Great Physician, and never let go till we are perfectly healed.

"With His stripes we are healed." Through the instrumentality of the sufferings of the Lord Jesus Christ, we are cured. The atonement He made is God's great instrument of curing us, for there would be no spiritual cure found regarding anyone all over the world, were it not for the atonement of Christ. But through pondering more and more what He did and suffered in our room and stead, by little and little we become more and more free from sin, by little and little we become more and more cured. He has apprehended us for the purpose of curing us, and He will not let us go till we are perfectly cured-that means, till we are as spotless, as holy, as free from sin, and as heavenly-minded as He Himself is, and as He Himself was in His life here on earth. And we should lay hold on this by faith. It is very difficult to enter into it; nay, it is completely impossible to enter into it by nature; and even at the beginning of the divine life it is very difficult to do so. I found it myself thus when I was converted 71 years and 6 months since, on account of the evil habits I had contracted. It was exceedingly difficult to put them aside. I had been passionately fond of the theatre, and was there day after day. I had been found at the ball-room, and at the card-table, and again and again at a late hour at the latter. And when I was converted, though I never touched a pack of cards again, though it was all over with the theatre, though I never went any more to the ball-room, yet these evil habits, these evil natural tendencies, were very difficult to surmount. I began to pray that God would give me power and victory over them; but, after I had been praying a good while, it appeared as if I never should lose my love for these things, as if continually they would come back to my mind and desire. But by little and little, after all, I got complete victory over them!

I mention this for the encouragement of young Christians, so that they may on no account despair and suppose they will not be able to withstand these things, and that they will not be able to live for the glory and honour of God. The Lord Jesus is your Physician. The Lord Jesus has taken you under His care. You are in the spiritual hospital of "the Great Physician," the Lord Jesus, and He is ready to help you. Look at Him! Expect great things from Him! "Open your mouth wide, and He will fill it." That is it. He will answer your prayers regarding the things that you require. O the blessedness of the position in which we stand as believers. Everyone of us who is trusting in the Lord Jesus Christ for salvation, who is born again, who has obtained spiritual life, shall at the last be perfectly holy! O the blessedness of this! We shall be completely heavenly-minded, so that throughout eternity never a command will go forth on the part of God that we shall do this, or another thing, but instantaneously the heart will say, "I delight, my Father, to do Thy will." And with the greatest alacrity we shall carry out the will of God; there will be no tardiness, no hesitation, no questioning in ourselves, whether we shall do it or not. But, as quickly as the command goes forth, we shall be ready to carry out His will.

For all this we are apprehended by God in Christ Jesus. We shall not be discharged out of the hospital of the Great Physician as incurable persons, but shall be made perfectly Christ-like in the end. This is what is brought before us here when it is said, "With His stripes we are healed." The cure having been begun, you, my brethren and sisters beloved, and I, shall be as holy in the end as the Lord Jesus Christ was while on earth! We have not attained to it yet, but the work is going on, and we shall attain to it hereafter, when the Lord has taken us home to Himself.

"All we like sheep." Notice here in the first place particularly that it is not only this one, and that one, who went like a sheep astray, but all, all; ALL-without exception. "All we like sheep have gone astray." And it must come, with everyone of us who desires to enter heaven, to this: that in our inmost soul we are able to reiterate this, and to say to God, "Thus it is that I, a guilty sinner, went astray." Every one who supposes that he is good, or that she is good, and that they deserve the favour of God because they have not been bad, but good, excellent people, are in the greatest error.

They think, on the ground of their own goodness, to go to heaven at last. On the ground of our own goodness, we can go to hell! But there is not among the innumerable multitude of the glorified spirits one single individual who got there on the ground of his or her own goodness; for, I repeat it, on the ground of our own goodness we can only go to hell, and not to heaven. We have no goodness of our own. There is nothing, nothing, NOTHING of goodness in us by nature, but everything which is contrary to the mind of God! And the worst of it all is we do not even see it is so bad-that it, in our natural condition. But there is the fact; the Word of God declares it. We have only to read the first three chapters of the Epistle of Paul to the Romans, and the second chapter of the Epistle of Paul to the Ephesians, and there is abundant proof how it is with us naturally.

But though thus with us, that like sheep we went astray and everyone turned to his own way, yet there is hope, yet there is hope, in regard to the salvation of our souls. For the greatest transgressor, for the oldest transgressor, if only he will accept what God has provided for us in the Person of the Lord Jesus Christ, there is hope, and none need despair. "We have turned everyone to his own way." Notice this particularly-"his own way." That is the great sin. It is not that everyone is a drunkard, or that everyone is a thief, or that everyone is habitually given to speaking nothing but lies. That may not be at all the case. There are persons who in their whole life have never drunk more than they ought to have done, who have never been guilty of taking away from anyone as much as the value of a pin that did not belong to them; indeed, their whole life and deportment, in a variety of ways, may be not at all outwardly bad. But this is our sin: that by nature we go our own way, instead of going God's way; and we live to please ourselves, instead of living to please God, and doing His work as we should. Doing our own work, pleasing ourselves, going our own way-this is the great sin of which everyone of the human family by nature is guilty. And we must come to see this! If we do not, we shall have no comfort whatever regarding heaven being our place and portion.

But while it is stated, and perfectly true is it regarding us, that like sheep we went astray, that every one turned to his own way, it is added, "And Jehovah hath laid on Him the iniquity of us all," O how precious the comfort! Had this not been added, I should not have had a particle of comfort in my own soul! I could have had no prospect with regard to heaven and glory at the last. But it is added, and added for everyone of us, the weakest and feeblest believers, a Jehovah hath laid on Him the iniquity of us all." For my habitually going to the theatre to amuse myself; for my going to the ball-room; for my being found at the card-table, sometimes to twelve at night-yea, once to two o'clock in the morning-for this my precious Lord Jesus was punished. That I thus misspent my time, that I thus misspent my faculties and my money, everything with which God had entrusted me as a steward; that I lived to myself, pleased myself; that in travelling I sought happiness, instead of seeking happiness in the Lord Jesus-for all this my precious Lord Jesus was punished. He did willingly, worthily bear the punishment; and now I, putting my trust in Him, am a forgiven sinner; and thus my brethren and sisters in Christ, doing the like, are forgiven ones. O how precious!

Now our business is to lay hold on this; to appropriate all this to ourselves; to write our very own name to these two verses, and say to ourselves, "Jehovah has laid on MY Lord Jesus Christ MY iniquity, as MY substitute, and has made Him to pay MY sins by death; and THEY have been perfectly paid, there is not found one single sin in ME unforgiven, and MY Heavenly Father is most perfectly satisfied with what MY adorable Lord Jesus Christ has done for ME, and has done for the countless multitude believing in Him." This is the conclusion of the whole. O how delightful it is to be able to appropriate all this to ourselves. Let not my young brethren and sisters say, "O this was very well regarding Isaiah, and such men as Daniel, and Jeremiah, and the Apostles; but that does not apply to me." Yes, it does apply to you, my weak brother and sister, my young brother and sister; it applies to everyone of us trusting in the Lord Jesus Christ alone for salvation. The sin that is in us has been perfectly punished, perfectly atoned for; and not a single sin at the last will be brought against us. Therefore afresh we should give thanks to God for His unspeakable gift, and rejoice in Christ Jesus, with deep gratitude for what God has done for us in Him!

Chapter 14: Paul's Thorn in the Flesh.

A Sermon preached on Sunday evening, July 11th, 1897, at Bethesda Chapel, Great George Street, Bristol.

2 Cor. 12:7,8,9.

THE POSITION IN which the Apostle Paul stood was that though, with his might, he had sought to do everything he could for the church at Corinth, through false teachers, who had crept in unawares, he was calumniated, spoken against, looked down upon, rejected, and the like; and he was under the painful necessity, for the sake of the Gospel and for the glory of God, to speak about himself in a manner which he had never done before, to justify himself before these adversaries of the Gospel. And this is frequently the case, not merely with preachers of the Gospel and pastors of churches, but with children of God generally, that they are evil spoken of. "For I suppose I was not a whit behind the very chiefest apostles."

After reading to the end of verse 27, chapter 11, Mr. Muller went on to remark: Just think of it, that this holy man, one of the holiest men that ever lived on earth, had to suffer from hunger and thirst, in fastings often, in cold and nakedness," being in the position that he could not have a comfortable place, being without in the cold, and with not sufficient warm clothing. "Besides those things that are without, that which cometh upon me daily, the care of all the churches. Who is weak, and I am not weak? . . . If I must needs glory, I will glory in the things which concern mine infirmities. The God and Father of our Lord Jesus Christ, which is blessed for evermore, knoweth that I lie not."

Commenting on the first six verses of the 12th chapter, Mr. Muller said: He Himself was the person, but he does not say so; though it is obvious that he was the person. "Of such an one will I glory: yet of myself I will not glory, but in mine infirmities"-that is, he could have mentioned far more than this, but he would no longer speak about himself, lest any should form too high an opinion of him, which he did not wish to be the case.

"Lest I 'should be exalted above measure, through the abundance of the revelations, there was given to me a thorn in the flesh, the messenger of Satan to buffet me, lest I should be exalted above measure. For this thing I besought the Lord thrice, that it might depart from me; and He said unto me, 'My grace is sufficient for thee, for My strength is made perfect in weakness.' Most gladly therefore will I rather glory in my infirmities, that the power of Christ may rest upon me. Therefore I take pleasure in infirmities, in reproaches, in necessities, in persecutions, in distresses, for Christ's sake, for when I am weak, then am I strong". "The confession of this holy man regarding his entire dependence on God, and his own weakness, yea nothingness, is especially to be treasured up in our own hearts, and we have to seek for grace to imitate him, in coming to the conclusion to which he came. "Lest I should be exalted above measure, through the abundance of the revelations." Notice here, how this most holy man, the chief of all the apostles, had such a view regarding himself that he considered he was in danger of being "exalted above measure, through the abundance of the revelations;" through what God had done for him in taking him to Paradise, in taking him, who was yet in the body, to be in a place which was only fit for those who were no longer in the body. He tells us that he was in danger of being "exalted above measure."

Now, if such a man of God as he was, "the chief of all the apostles," the one who, in honesty of heart, could say about himself that he had "laboured more abundantly" than any of the apostles-if he could confess that he was in danger of being "exalted above measure," what shall we weak ones, and feeble ones, in comparison with the Apostle Paul, say regarding ourselves? Most assuredly, if with any measure of truth and of uprightness of heart we have to make a confession regarding ourselves, we must say, "If Paul was in danger of being exalted above measure, a thousand times more may we be in danger of being exalted above measure, and of having too high an opinion about ourselves."

Now, then, the remedy was provided, even for Paul, regarding this. "Lest I should be exalted above measure, through the abundance of the revelations, there was given to me a thorn in the flesh"-that is, a trial, and a very heavy trial, to counterbalance, that he might not be "exalted above measure." We are not told what this thorn in the flesh was. That it was something very painful, very trying, we see by the figure which is used. Many of us may know from our own experience what it is to have a little splinter, or thorn, go into our hands, or any part of our body; how painful it is until the thorn, or the little splinter, is extracted-how exceedingly painful it is. Therefore, it was something extremely painful on purpose, we have reason to believe. We are not told what it was, for if we had been told such a thing, or such a thing, or such a thing, then those who were not similarly situated might say, "O this might be borne," or, "I could have borne it." So, in order that none of us might say regarding ourselves, "O my trial is a different one, and a far heavier one," we purposely are not informed what this thorn in the flesh was.

But evidently, by the very figure which is used, it was something extremely trying that he had to bear day by day, week after week, month after month. This thorn in the flesh is called, "The messenger of Satan," because through the instrumentality of Satan came the trial. All trials that come upon us, in our family, in our business, in our health, and in other ways, come directly, or indirectly, through the instrumentality of the Wicked One. Our Heavenly Father tries to make us pass through this life pleasantly, easily, happily, without having trials and afflictions; but Satan hates us, exceedingly hates us, because he knows that we are no longer belonging to his kingdom-we who put our trust in the Lord Jesus Christ for salvation. We no longer belong to him.

That he will not have us at last for eternity, to torment us, to make us wretched and miserable, he knows; and therefore, as he cannot have us then, he seeks to make us in this life, while we are in the body, as unhappy as he possibly can. He tries to afflict us, to torment us, to the very uttermost that he has permission to do; for we have ever to keep before us that he can do nothing against us, unless he obtains first permission from God. A most striking illustration of this we have in the case of Job. Satan had been trying to get at him, but was unable to do so; he had been trying to injure him, his family, his property, but he could not do so, and he was constrained to make a confession, "Hast Thou not set a hedge round about him?" That is, he had often and often unquestionably tried to get at Job, but could not by reason of the protection which God gave to His holy servant. And therefore he says, "Thou hast set a hedge round about him," which implies, "I have often tried to get at him, but I was unable to do so." And this hedge is never broken down, except by the permission of God. A wall of fire is round about us, and Satan dare not touch us, except God gives permission; and this permission is never, never, NEVER given, except God has determined to rule it all for the confounding of Satan, and for our real good and blessing and comfort. So that we come under this precious promise, "All things work together for good to them that love God."

If Satan is permitted to break down the hedge, this permission is only given for the purpose of confounding him, and of bringing more blessing to us out of it than if the hedge were not broken. O how precious the position of the children of God! And if everyone knew what it means to be a child of God, everyone most earnestly would seek to become a child of God. But because it is not known, we are naturally blinded, we have no proper Scriptural idea of what it implies to be a child of God; therefore we care not about it, we treat the matter with indifference. But all those who are made to see their lost and ruined condition by nature, all those who have turned to find out, in any goodly measure, that they are sinners, and that they deserve nothing but punishment, and who own this before God in prayer, and then put their trust in the Lord Jesus Christ for the salvation of their souls, become happy, happy, happy beings. They are blessed, and truly blessed, and no other persons are really and truly blessed and really and truly happy until they come to this!

Therefore, should there be any here present who have not found out yet that they are sinners, great sinners, deserving nothing but punishment, let them pray to God that He will be pleased, in the riches of His grace, to show it to them, and when they have come to see it, then humble themselves before God, make confession of their sinfulness before Him, and ask His merciful forgiveness. When they are come as far as this, they have further to put their trust alone in Jesus Christ for the salvation of their souls. Being brought thus far, they are regenerated; through this trust in the Lord Jesus Christ they become a new creation, they become children of God, they obtain spiritual life, they are now born again, they belong no longer to the world, and they stand as justified ones before God, through the righteousness of the Lord Jesus, and they are forgiven ones by reason of the atonement which the Lord Jesus Christ made in their room and stead. For He not only fulfilled the law, He also bore its punishment, and on this account we shall not be condemned, because the Lord Jesus Christ bore all the punishment which we guilty sinners ought to have borne; and this belongs not merely to one or the other, not merely to a few thousands of human beings, but belongs to every one whose eyes have been spiritually opened to see his lost condition, and who really has trusted in Jesus for salvation. Now, being brought on the road to heaven, having obtained spiritual life, as assuredly as we continue putting our trust alone in Jesus Christ, we shall at last reach glory.

"There was given to me a thorn in the flesh, the messenger of Satan, to buffet me." This figure is particularly to be noticed. "Beats me with his fists," that is the literal meaning of "to buffet me." "Beats me with his fists." This figure implies the greatness of the trial, the greatness of the suffering, that he had to endure from this "messenger of Satan," from this evil angel, this evil spirit. And this buffeting was, " Lest I should be exalted above measure"-that is, God allows it in order that on no account the Apostle Paul should be exalted; that he might be kept in real, true humility of soul, that he might have a lowly view about himself. Now let us not forget this, that if such an exceedingly holy man as was the Apostle Paul was in danger of being "exalted above measure on account of the abundance of the revelations" which he had had, how much more is this the case regarding ourselves? Now, what did this man of God do under these circumstances? "For this thing I besought the Lord thrice, that it might depart from me."

Because this "messenger of Satan" was so very trying, the sufferings were so exceedingly great, he, with earnestness, besought God that it might be taken from him. When it is stated here he "besought the Lord thrice," he did not for five minutes ask God three times, but we have reason to believe it means in a solemn way, most earnestly, at three different times he besought the Lord that it might depart from him. This is what we have to do, to come to the Lord under trial and affliction, and beseech Him to take it away. And if the prayer, once prayed before God, is not enough, to bring it the second time, to bring it the third time, to bring it the thirtieth time, to bring it the fiftieth time before the Lord, until we plainly see that He has something better for us, and therefore does not take it away. But until we are instructed about this, we may go on praying that God graciously would take away the heavy trial, the heavy affliction.

Now, in the 9th verse we see what the Lord Himself says, "And He said unto me, 'My grace is sufficient for thee, for My strength is made perfect in weakness.'" Grace is sufficient for every trial and every affliction, because, obtaining grace, we get the Holy Spirit as the Comforter, as the Strengthener, of the inner life, the divine life, the spiritual life we have obtained; and He leads us on spiritually and helps us under all circumstances, under all trials, under all afflictions, of whatever character they may be. Therefore the great point is this, "Are we partakers of grace?" Then, and only then, have we obtained spiritual life. Only then are we regenerated, only then are we warranted to look at ourselves as the children of God, and as pardoned sinners through faith in the Lord Jesus Christ. O how precious is this, that as partakers of grace we are helped for time and for eternity. When once brought to this, we are no longer in nature's darkness, we no longer belong to the kingdom of Satan, but to the kingdom of God. We then are the children of God, and as such the heirs of God, and joint-heirs with the Lord Jesus Christ. We then for eternity have the Lord Jesus as our Friend, as our Helper, as our Comforter, as our Guide, as our Counsellor, and as the One Who will watch over us and never leave us or hide Himself away from us, in order that He may shield and protect us against the powers of darkness. O the blessedness of such a position!

Now I ask, before going any further, "Are you partakers of this grace?" I have been through the wondrous mercy of God, in this state to which I have referred, for 71 years and 8 months. And as God has bestowed this wondrous blessing on me, He is willing to bestow it on anyone who is yet without peace. We must obtain this blessing if we desire to go to heaven at last! There is no such thing as obtaining this blessing when once we have passed out of time into eternity. In the world to come there is no seeking after Christ; in the world to come there is no such thing as being regenerated; in the world to come there is no such thing as obtaining forgiveness for our sins, if we do not obtain forgiveness before passing out of time into eternity! Now, then, ask yourselves, I beseech and entreat all of you who are not certain on Scriptural grounds that you have obtained the blessing-ask yourselves, "How is it with me, and shall I still go on without this blessing, and treat it yet with indifference as I have done for a long time?" O, on no account delay to care about your souls. The present moment is ours, and the present moment alone is ours. How it may be after a single hour, who will tell us? Often, often it has happened that persons who were at a religious meeting were one hour afterwards no longer in the land of the living. Now, I do not say that this will be the case with any here present to-night; but because of the possibility, therefore let us, on no account, delay to care about our souls.

"My grace is sufficient for thee." Paul had obtained grace; that meant in every position in life that he could need it, though he had "the thorn in the flesh," grace was given to him to counteract. Though he had "the messenger of Satan" sent to him, yet grace could counteract this. Though he was "beaten with fists," greatly afflicted, greatly tried, yet grace was sufficient to meet all. "My grace is sufficient for thee, for My strength is made perfect in weakness." That means "My power is just seen more abundantly on account of thy weakness; thou art a weak one in thyself, thou hast no strength in thyself, but the power is Mine, and My power shall be made manifest in thy weakness." Now, what decision did Paul come to, when this was told him? "Most gladly therefore will I rather glory in mine infirmities, that the power of Christ may rest upon me." "I will no longer be tried, though I have this 'thorn in the flesh;' I will no longer be tried by 'this messenger of Satan to buffet me;' I will rejoice rather than be tried, by reason of what I have, through the grace of God, to strengthen me."

"Most gladly therefore will I rather glory in mine infirmities, that the power of Christ may dwell in me," for this is the meaning of to "rest upon me." Dwell in me, that I may be a partaker of the power of Christ, through the grace bestowed on me. We weak ones, and feeble ones, may therefore say to ourselves, "In myself I am extremely weak, in myself I am nothing, I can do nothing, I have no power of my own; but the power of Christ dwells in me, through the Holy Ghost being given to me." O how precious! And the Holy Spirit we have individually, as assuredly as we have owned before God that we are sinners, and trusted in the Lord Jesus Christ for the salvation of our souls. That brings this wondrous blessing to us, and the power of Christ dwells in us, in the gift of the Holy Spirit.

"Therefore I take pleasure in infirmities, in reproaches, in necessities, in persecutions, in distresses for Christ's sake, for when I am weak, then am I strong." See what effect this had had upon the Apostle Paul, when once he knew that the very way of obtaining great blessing, exceeding great blessing, was just the position in which he was, because he was a partaker of the grace of God, and that therefore he should never be left nor forsaken! He could then come to the conclusion, "I take pleasure in infirmities." "Take pleasure in infirmities"-that is, when weak in body he took pleasure in his weakness, because the power of Christ dwelt in him. "I take pleasure in reproaches." He was called "a fool," "a madman," "a good-far-nothing fellow," "not fit to live; " these reproaches were heaped upon him, but the Apostle Paul now says, "I take pleasure in these reproaches; yea, though men reproach me, to make me wretched and miserable, they only make me happy by the reproaches which they heap upon me, because I know what blessing all this in the end will bring." Then, he further says,

"I take pleasure in necessities." When I am hungry, when I have not sufficient food, when I have no proper clothing to warm and to shield me against the inclemencies of the weather, or, when in other respects, I am in necessities, I take pleasure in them, because I now see that this is the very opportunity given to the Lord Jesus Christ, Who by the power of His Spirit dwells in me, and this power dwells in me to help me, to comfort me, and to bring a blessing to my soul.

In persecutions he could now take pleasure. No longer complaining of being dissatisfied because he was persecuted, but taking pleasure in it, because it gave to the Lord Jesus Christ an opportunity of manifesting His power. Then he says, "I take pleasure in distresses, for Christ's sake." Not in distresses on account of having acted improperly, imprudently, but for the sake of the Lord Jesus Christ. If he were in distress he would take pleasure in it, for it would bring blessing to his soul. And the whole is wound up with this, "For when I am weak, then am I strong;" because of the power of the Lord Jesus Christ dwelling in him. Now, our comfort is particularly this, that these glorious statements referred not merely to such an one as the Apostle Paul was, but they refer to the weakest, feeblest, least instructed child of God; yea, they belong to the new-born babe in Christ who but this morning was brought to the knowledge of Jesus Christ. O how precious is all this; and when we appropriate these things to ourselves, we are no longer cast down, we become peaceful and happy, very peaceful and very happy, We glory in the greatest trials and difficulties, because we see they are all appointed for our good and blessing and profit, and they all give to the Lord Jesus Christ the opportunity of manifesting His power in reference to ourselves. They give Him also an opportunity of manifesting His matchless care and love, which He has for the weakest and feeblest of His children.

Now our business is to enter into all this, and if, as yet we are unable to do so, to ask the Lord to strengthen us, by His Holy Spirit, that we may comprehend all that which is contained in these few verses on which we have now meditated; and, in doing so, lasting, lasting and abiding blessing will come to our souls.

Chapter 15: Glorying in the Cross of Christ.

A Sermon preached at Bethesda Chapel, Great George Street, Bristol, on Sunday evening, March 14th, 1897.

Gal. 6:14.

THIS VERSE WAS written by the Apostle Paul in contradistinction to the false teachers, who gloried, made their boast, and rejoiced in outward observances, outward forms and ceremonies, and in all the Mosaic appointments which were intended only for a time, until there came the Saviour of sinners, our Lord Jesus. Now in contradistinction to these false teachers the Apostle writes, "But God forbid;" that means, "Far be it." That is always the meaning when we find this phrase, either in the Old or the New Testament. "But 'far be it' that I should glory"-that I, the Apostle Paul, should glory, make my boast, rejoice in this, as those false teachers did-" 'far be it' that I should glory save in the cross of our Lord Jesus Christ." In the cross of the Lord Jesus Christ he would glory, make his boast, rejoice!

Now the first thing that we have to ask is, "What is meant by the CROSS of Christ?" Not the ceremonies of the Papists, in crossing themselves, that is not the meaning of it; nor to wear, as an ornament, a cross; nor to carry about a large construction representing the cross on which the Lord Jesus Christ hung and was put to death; nor does it mean that cross on which He expired, was hanged, and His hands and feet pierced with large nails-for if it were possible that we could have that very identical cross, it would not be worth a farthing; it could do no good whatever. Relics were sold in Popish times, and alleged relics of this very identical cross on which the Lord Jesus Christ hung have been sold for very large sums of money. But all of no use. If the whole of the identical cross on which the Lord Jesus Christ was put to death could be obtained, it would profit nothing- as to the salvation of the soul; it would profit nothing even as to one particle of spiritual benefit to be derived from it; it would be worth not one single farthing so far as the actual value was concerned in reference to spiritual benefit.

Now, then, what have we to understand by the cross of Christ? Even this. The blessing obtained through the instrumentality of what our precious Lord Jesus Christ accomplished while He was hanging on the cross, shedding His blood for the salvation of our souls! This is what we have to understand by the cross of Christ! Now nothing in which these false teachers glory, in which they make their boast, is of the least particle of spiritual profit and avail; but that which our Lord Jesus Christ accomplished while He hung on the cross, shedding His blood for the remission of our sins, making an atonement for us, delivering us from the curse of the law, this is of the deepest value! O how precious! Now this we have particularly to keep before us! When the Lord Jesus Christ hung on the cross, it was that He might make an atonement for our sins! It was that He might bear the punishment due to all who put their trust in Him! It was that He might deliver us from the curse of the law, because He became thus a curse for us, for it is written in the Books of Moses that "He who hangs on a tree," i.e., is put to death as a malefactor by being bung on a tree, "is accursed of God;" and it was by the Lord Jesus Christ thus worthily allowing Himself to be put to death by wicked men on the tree, and on the cross, that He delivered us from the curse of the law.

Every sinner in his natural state is a transgressor before God! Everyone, so long as he or she is not a believer in the Lord Jesus Christ, is under the curse of God, by day and by night, whether at home, or travelling, whether on the land or on the sea, whether eating or fasting, whether at work or at rest-all the time that he is not a believer in the Lord Jesus Christ he is under the curse of God! Every morsel he puts into his mouth, he puts there as one who is accursed of God; every drop of water he takes, he takes as one who is under the curse of God. And wherever he is, in whatever state of body, in whatever occupation he is engaged, he is under the curse, so long as he is not a believer in the Lord Jesus Christ!

O remember this! And in this state we must remain until we are believers in the Lord Jesus, for we have no righteousness of our own by which we can commend ourselves to God! There is no righteousness of our own that will deliver us from this curse under which we are by nature! A fearful condition in which every unconverted person is, and it is simply because they do not see it that they have a particle of quietness of mind; that they are not raving mad is simply because they are ignorant of the condition in which they are! O the solemnity of the thought! Can it be too much weighed, too much considered, too much pondered, in order to get rid of it?

Then, again, through the cross of the Lord Jesus we are not simply delivered from the curse; through what the Lord Jesus Christ worthily took on Himself to deliver us from, the state in which we are by nature, we are not merely delivered, but from the state of thraldom and slavery of sin in which all of us are as unconverted. Spiritual freedom we only receive, and can only receive, by putting our trust in the Lord Jesus, by apprehending the power of the Blood of Christ, shed by Him when He made an atonement for our sins, hanging on the accursed tree! O the solemnity of this! We try to make ourselves better in our natural condition, we try to put aside this thing and another thing, which we see to be contrary to the mind of God. We may have in our natural condition light enough to see that we cannot remain in the condition in which we are; and try then, on this account, to make ourselves better, but we are unable to deliver ourselves from the slavery and bondage of sin till we are brought to believe in Christ.

O, I remember sometimes as a young man, being from my earliest days educated to become a clergyman, and yet careless, reckless, unconcerned about the things of God, never reading the Scriptures, going on in all the folly and frivolity of this present evil world, caring only about eating and drinking, new clothes, and going about to the theatre, the ball-room, to the card-table, and the billiard-room, All these things I only cared about, not about God and His precious Word. Under these circumstances, nevertheless twice a year, the Lord's Supper was taken, as a formal thing, a customary thing; and twice at such times I swore with the bread of the ordinance in my mouth that I would become a different man, for I had light enough to see that it would not do to go on in this careless way, habitually frequenting the theatre, and the ball-room, and the card-table, and the billiard-room-it would not do to become a clergyman under such circumstances. Therefore, I swore solemnly twice on these occasions I would become different. The next day was just as before.

How came this? Not because there was not a measure of sincerity. I saw the folly in a certain sense of going on in this way, but I was dead in trespasses and in sins. I had no spiritual life in myself. I was not regenerated. Therefore, I was a ready victim to the devil; he could lead me about, and induce me just as he pleased, and bid me do this, that, or another thing, and I was ready enough to do it by reason of the natural, carnal mind. But the moment I apprehended the power of the Blood of Christ, I became completely different. One evening, at a little prayer meeting, I saw, all at once, by the grace of God, that I was a sinner, and that Christ was a Saviour for sinners, and having entered the house where the little meeting was held as one who was as far from God as he possibly could be, I left a happy Christian.

That night I found myself lying on my bed peacefully, a forgiven sinner, and without a single human being having conversed with me on the subject. I said at once to my Heavenly Father, "My Heavenly Father, I no longer go to the theatre, I no longer go to the ball-room, I no longer shall be found at the card-table, and in the billiard-room; I know something far better than these; Thou hast made me to be a happy child of Thine; I seek now to live to Thee, to glorify Thee." This without having conversed with a single individual under heaven. I was at once instructed by the Holy Ghost to say this to my Heavenly Father. I became now a spiritually free man. Before, I was a slave to sin for 20 years and five weeks. Now, being a believer in Christ, regenerated, born again, a child of God, all was at an end, and ever since that time, on the 1st of November, 1825, now 71 years ago, my whole life has been a different one.

Now, you see the oath that I had sworn to God came to nothing, simply because I was not born again; I was not a believer in Christ. I had depended in my own strength to make myself different, and all came to nothing; but when I came to Christ, was made a believer in the Lord Jesus Christ, I became a spiritually free man, and I obtained thus, through faith in Christ, power over sin, because I had now spiritual life, and I was constrained by love and gratitude to the precious Lord Jesus Christ to live a completely different life from what before had been the case. Now, then, this brings before us that we should glory in the cross of Christ, that we should make our boast in the cross of Christ, that we should rejoice in what the Lord Jesus Christ did for sinners while He hung on the cross, because He made an atonement for their sins, and thus obtained for them that they should become spiritually free men. Through faith in Him they are regenerated, obtain spiritual life, and thus become free from sin.

Now let us particularly seek to enter into this, that we should glory in the cross of Christ, make our boast in it. We have no goodness of our own, no merit of our own, no righteousness of our own; our good acts and deeds are compared to filthy rags in the Scriptures-there is sin connected with them all; therefore in our own goodness, merit, worthiness, and righteousness we cannot make our boast. But in what the Lord Jesus Christ has done for poor sinners, and is doing for poor sinners, we can glory and make our boast, because it becomes ours through faith in the Lord Jesus Christ!

Firstly, all the glory belongs to God, not the least particle of glory belongs to us; what we are, and what we have, we have all in and through our Lord Jesus Christ; we have nothing in ourselves. The Lord Jesus Christ, through what He has accomplished, has given us spiritual life! We, who were dead in trespasses and in sins, have obtained through faith in Him spiritual life. And let me affectionately tell all those who are not yet believers in the Lord Jesus Christ, who are dead in trespasses and sins. "You have no spiritual life in yourselves, you can have no spiritual life in yourselves, till you are believers in the Lord Jesus Christ; and therefore, being dead in trespasses and sins, you cannot make yourselves better, because you are dead, and just as a dead man cannot make himself better, so you cannot make yourselves better as long as you are not believers in Christ." Therefore ask God to show you that you are sinners, that you may own it before God in prayer; and then when you have owned it before God, ask Him to help you to put your trust in the Lord Jesus Christ for salvation, for so you will obtain spiritual life, being born again.

Through this faith in the Lord Jesus Christ we obtain forgiveness of our sins: every one of our numberless transgressions is forgiven, immediately forgiven, when we believe in the Lord Jesus Christ. We cannot work in any way so as to obtain this forgiveness by our own doings, by our own work. It is through Jesus having made an atonement for our sins that we obtain forgiveness; it is through Jesus having in our room and stead fulfilled the law of God, the commandments of God, that we, putting our trust in Him, are reckoned righteous. For naturally we are unrighteous, we are sinners, and great sinners in the sight of God. But the believer in Christ is pardoned, and everyone of his numberless transgressions forgiven; not a single sin remains to be punished, but everyone forgiven! Now, is not this unspeakably blessed? O seek to enter into it! It is this which makes me such a happy man!

I know that though I have been guilty of thousands and tens of thousands of sins, in action, in word, in thought, in feeling, in desire, in purpose, in inclination, yet everyone of these thousands and tens of thousands of sins is forgiven, and not one single sin stands against me. So I am able to look my Heavenly Father in the face without dread and without fear; I would follow Him up to the end of my earthly pilgrimage, either by death or the return of the Lord Jesus Christ, and I look at all this without a particle of dread or fear, because, as a believer in Christ, all my numberless transgressions are forgiven. I am regenerated through faith in Christ, and thus have I become a child of God, and the Lord Jesus Christ my Elder Brother. I am an heir of God and a joint-heir with Christ! O how precious are all these things.

And hereafter, as regards the world to me, my prospect is I shall have a glorified body and I shall be perfectly like what the Lord Jesus Christ was while here on earth! O how precious these prospects are! In body like the Lord Jesus after His resurrection, in spirit, in soul, like Him, when I see Him as He is. Perfectly holy! O how precious this; and thus it will go on throughout eternity, one thousand years after the other. Unspeakably happy in the presence of God! One thousand years after the other, partaking of the "rivers of pleasure at the right hand of God!" Not a few draughts of pleasure! Notice the figure. The "rivers of pleasure." The rivers of pleasure, in order to bring before the poor sinner who trusts in Christ what awaits him! How unspeakably blessed the prospect of eternity is!

O if we entered into it, everyone would at once come to the Lord Jesus; but because these things are considered simply as religious frenzies and not as realities, they are treated with indifference and carelessness, and put off for a while; and persons say to themselves, "Hereafter I may think a little more about it, but at present I will enjoy the world." And thus, day after day, and week after week, these blessed, glorious realities are put aside, until suddenly one day the end comes and the sinner is found in an unprepared state! O if this were only entered into! One thousand years after the other, one million years after the other, one hundred millions of years after the other, and all these enjoyments in the presence of the Lord, the partaking of the "rivers of pleasure," of never-ending delights! O if this were taken seriously, persons would indeed care about their souls!

Now the last sentence of our passage. "Far be it from me that I should glory save in the cross of our Lord Jesus Christ." We see the results of this in what follows, "By whom the world is crucified unto me and I unto the world." By entering into what the Lord Jesus Christ has done for us, the result is this. First, the heart is filled with love and gratitude to God for the gift of Jesus, and to the precious Jesus for giving Himself in our room and stead. Next, we are regenerated, become children of God, obtain spiritual life, heavenly life, become one with Christ, and are thus filled with love and gratitude to the precious Jesus for what He accomplished in our room and stead. And the result of this is, in this life, that we in spirit are separated from the world, we can no longer go on in their ways, in their habits, in their maxims, just as I stated was the result in my own case. The very first evening I was brought to Christ, the theatre was given up, the ballroom was given up, the card-table was given up, the billiard-table put aside, and all the worldly habits in which I had been going on year after year; and my heart longed to live a completely different life. Thus, in spirit, separated from the world, completely separated; and what was the result of this? The world separated also from me.

I remember so well my fellow-students. I was at the University at the time, where there were 1,200 young men, and they knew what a thorough comrade I had been in all their ways, their habits and maxims, and they laughed at me, they pointed their fingers at me, "There goes the fool!" "There goes the madman!" "There goes the enthusiast!" This is what they said. I, in heart and spirit, separated from the world; and they, because of my godly ways, separated themselves from me. Thus it is everywhere with true children of God. They can no longer go on as they used to go on, and the world will no longer reckon them as being one with themselves. They separate from the world, and the world separates from them. They no longer caring about the things of the world, the world no longer cares about them, any more than they would care about a crucified malefactor hanging on the cross. This is the result on both sides where it is really Christ in the heart. Separation from the world comes where it is really Christ in the heart, in the life, and deportment. The world does not care about such; the world turns its back upon them. He is a fool, an enthusiast, a madman, a fanatic, and the world will have nothing to do with him.

Now, one word more. How is it with us who are professed disciples of the Lord Jesus? Have we really come out from among the world? Are we really walking in separation from the world? Is the world crucified to us-that is, no more valued by us than a malefactor hanging on the cross? And on the other hand, is our life and deportment of that character that the world has turned its back on us just as we have turned our backs on the world? Does the world care no more about us than it would care about a malefactor hanging on the cross? That is the meaning, "The world is crucified unto us and we are crucified unto the world."

Now let us seek to know more and more in secret meditation how unspeakably precious it is to be a believer in Christ. Let us seek to be found more and more in secret, meditating on what the Lord Jesus Christ has done in our room and stead, in order that our hearts increasingly may be filled with gratitude and love to the Precious One; and particularly let our inmost soul be assured that we cannot save ourselves, that no goodness of ours can bring us to heaven. Our own goodness can only bring us to hell, not to heaven. For we have to own that all our goodness is, in the sight of God, as filthy rags-that is, our own righteousness. But if we are putting our trust in Christ, we are delivered from the curse. We are born again, we are spiritually free men, we have power with God; and power over sin through faith in Christ. God grant us this blessing.

Chapter 16: "Open thy mouth wide, and I will fill it."

A Sermon preached at the Gospel Hall, St. Nicholas Road, Bristol, on Sunday morning, January 10th, 1897.

Psalm 81:10.

THIS IS A figure we all understand, "Open thy mouth wide, and I will fill it;" that is, "Ask great blessings from Me, very great blessings, and I am ready to bestow them." O what a precious, glorious promise at the opening of the New Year, for poor weak ones, as we are. "Open thy mouth wide, and I will fill it." The great point is to apply this to our various particular positions, and to the circumstances in which we are placed.

We often find that the hindrance to the answer of prayer lies in ourselves, because our hearts are not yet prepared for a blessing. Now, in connection with this verse, "Open thy mouth wide, and I will fill it," I will refer, for the comfort and encouragement of beloved Christian friends, to my own experience in connection with the Orphan work, in order that you all increasingly may be comforted and encouraged to expect great things at the hands of God. It is now 68 years ago that my heart was greatly tried, when again and again I saw dear children losing both parents, and there was no one to take a real deep interest in their well-being.

I felt deeply for such bereaved children, and I said again and again to myself, "O I wish I had a little Orphan institution, into which I could take these children." But the desire remained for years only a desire, though I had much prayer in connection with it. In the November of the year 1835, a particular circumstance occurred, through the instrumentality of which I was made to know how to be able to do something for destitute orphans, and I began to pray more earnestly than ever I had done before that God would be pleased to guide and direct me whether I should make a beginning of a little Orphan institution. Thus I prayed month after month, and at last I came to the decision that I would do something in this way; and though it might have never so small a beginning, I would make a beginning.

After having come to this decision, I passed one evening-namely, on the 5th of November, 1835-reading the Scriptures, and, as my habit has been since July, 1829, going consecutively through them. That is, not picking out here and there a little portion and reading it, or a few verses here and there, or half a chapter here and there, but going on straight forward, through the whole of the Old Testament, and then through the New Testament. Then, having finished the whole of the Holy Bible, beginning again from the commencement, and so going on. This has been my habit now ever since July, 1829, and I have read four times every year through the whole Bible, with prayer and meditation, and especially with meditation in reference to myself. How does this comfort you? How does it instruct you? How does it warn you? How does it reprove and rebuke you? Thus do I read the Holy Scriptures in regard to myself.

Now, just reading through the whole Bible, I came, at that time, to this 81st Psalm and to this 10th verse, "I am Jehovah thy God, Who brought thee out of the land of Egypt: open thy mouth wide, and I will fill it." When I read this verse, I shut the Bible, went to the door of my room and locked it, and then I cast myself on the floor and began to pray. I said to my Heavenly Father, "I have only asked Thee, Heavenly Father, that Thou shouldest show me whether I shall begin the Orphan work or not. Thou hast been pleased to make that plan to me, and now 'I will open my mouth wide.' Be pleased to 'fill it.' Give me, my Heavenly Father, a suitable house to begin the work; give me suitable helpers to take care of the children; and give me a thousand pounds sterling to make a beginning.

A thousand pounds was a very great sum at that time. At the present day it is a very small sum for me, for often and often I have in one day to pay away -a thousand pounds? No, not merely a thousand, but £2,000, £3,000, in one day; yea, again and again £4,000, £5,000, and £6,000 in one day. But at that time a thousand pounds was a great sum to me. Nevertheless, I expected to get it, though I did not know how. I expected to get it from my Heavenly Father, on the ground of this promise. The next day I received a shilling from a German missionary staying in my house. I had for six months, staying with me, six missionaries, brethren and sisters, and one of these brethren gave me a shilling. Another German missionary staying in my house, out of the six, gave me another shilling. This was the first money I received in connection with the thousand pounds.

Everyone of you say, "A very little beginning;" but it was a beginning. I received also on the same day a second gift, a very large wardrobe for the house I was going to open for destitute orphans. Then I went on praying, and by little and little I received more; and very soon there was one especially remarkable answer to prayer. There was in fellowship with us a sister, a seamstress. She earned by her needle half-a-crown, or three shillings, or three-and-six; but the very utmost that now and then she earned was five shillings-never more than this. And this weakly, afflicted sister, this seamstress, sent me £100 for the Orphan work. I would not accept it. I knew not how this came about, that this poor, weakly sister, who earned so very little, should have sent me £100.

I therefore sent for her, and had an interview with her. I found that her grandfather had died, and by a legacy, in which he had left to his children and grandchildren, this money had come to her. The sum of £480 had been left to her, and out of this she would give £100 for the Orphan work. When I saw her, I said, "I cannot accept your £100, for I am afraid you have done all this in haste, and you may regret it afterwards, and that would be a sad affair. I cannot take this money." She said, "I have not done it in haste; I have well considered it; I have prayed much over it. I must entreat you to take the money. My brothers and sisters each gave to my mother £50, out of the money that they had inherited; but, as I am a believer in the Lord Jesus Christ, I gave my mother £100. Then my brothers and sisters would pay the debts of my father when he died, though they were not bound to do it; but they agreed with the creditors, the public-house keepers to whom he owed the money, for he was fond of drinking, that they would give five shillings in the pound.

"Now, though my father did not as he ought to have done, in incurring these debts at public-houses, yet he was my father, and I am a child of God, and I ought to honour my father, though he did not walk as he should have done, and I agreed with these public-house keepers that I would repay the whole of their debt. So I went and paid the fifteen shillings in the pound which my brothers and sisters had not paid. And you must take the £100. I feel so deeply interested in your purposing to open a little Orphan institution, that I would rather give the whole of the money than that it should not come to pass; and to show to you that I do it after much consideration, here is not merely the hundred pounds, but five pounds more, which I request you to give to the poor as a proof that I do this heartily, and have well considered it."

Under these circumstances, I saw how this godly sister had well weighed the matter, and I took the hundred pounds just as God's plan of giving. And thus by little and little, and with large help from some, came in the money, and I was able to open a large house in Wilson Street, in St. Paul's parish, with the extremely useful help of two sisters who gave themselves to the work, one as a teacher and the other as a seamstress. Thus I was able to fit up and furnish a house, and had a small sum in hand to make a beginning. The house was now ready, and a day was fixed when I would receive the applications for the reception of orphans. I went to the vestry. I had appointed two hours to see the relatives of destitute orphans. I sat there half-an-hour. Nobody came. I sat a whole hour. Nobody came. I sat an hour and a half. I sat two hours. Nobody came to make application for orphans, and I had to go away without one single application.

On my way home, I said to myself, "I have prayed about everything, but I have never asked God to send me orphans." For I took it for granted that there were tens, and hundreds, and thousands of orphans in England, and that the orphans would be coming in hundreds. But the Word of God says, "In everything by prayer and supplication, let your requests be made known to God." I had prayed for the right house, for the right helpers, for the money; and, when I had finished the house, I prayed about the furniture, almost every article. But I had never asked God to send orphans.

Well, I cast myself down on the floor before God, and confessed that I had erred in this matter, and asked His forgiveness, and asked Him if, after all, I had been deceiving myself, and that He would be more glorified by bringing the whole to nought than by my getting an Orphan institution to do so-to bring the whole thing to nought. If He could be more glorified, I should rejoice.

But I could not help thinking that it would be for the glory and honour of His Name if He brought it to pass, and I asked Him to send me orphans. The next morning, at eleven o'clock, I went again, and before one month had passed 42 orphans had applied, though the house was only large enough for 30. So God answered prayer, and the house was filled. Six months later I opened a second house for 36 children. That was filled very soon. Twelve months later I opened a third house for 30 children. That was filled, and a short time after I opened a fourth house for 30 more children. Now I had 126 orphans, with eleven helpers, who laboured among these children.

But the applications continued more and more. I therefore felt I must build a house, large enough to hold hundreds of orphans. But this would cost an immense sum of money. However, I said, "The Lord is able to give it to me," and for thirteen weeks I prayed for land. The Lord gave it me on Ashley Down. Then I continued praying for money, as I wanted to build a house for 300 orphans. By little and little it came in. I began the house. The house was finished. All was paid for, though it cost more than £15,000. Yet I had £676 over and above, after all was paid. But the house was soon filled, and the applications increased more and more.

Then I said, "Lord, what wilt Thou have me to do?" And after much prayer, it was to go on building accommodation for 700 more, that I might have 1,000 orphans under my care. Now, when I had nothing but £30 in hand, the devil said, and had it circulated, that I had £30,000 in hand. Instead of contradicting it in the newspapers, saying that it was a lie of Satan, I simply spoke to my Heavenly Father, "Lord, Thou knowest that this is a lie of Satan; confound him; Lord, confound him, and influence the hearts of Thy children to help me." So by little and little the money came in, and after a number of years there stood another house, and all paid for, and a third house for 350 more began!

That also was finished. Now I had accommodation for 1,150 orphans, and, after all was paid for, there were between two and three thousand pounds over and above in hand! But, remarkable to say, nine hundred orphans were yet waiting for admission! I had now accommodation for 1,150, but 900 were yet waiting. So I prayed, "Lord, what wilt Thou have me to do? I do not want orphan houses, but if Thou wilt help me to go on, here is Thy servant, and I am ready." Well, I began two houses more, each for 450, that I might be able to accommodate those 900 that were waiting, and there stood the houses after some years, erected at a cost of £60,000.

Now these five houses accommodate at one time 2,050 orphans, and I have accommodation for 112 helpers and assistants as matrons, teachers, etc., for the destitute orphans. *And in all God has been pleased to give me, simply in answer to prayer, £1,416,000 sterling! One million, four hundred and sixteen thousand pounds sterling, without asking a single human being! !*

There is none, in this whole city, who can say that I ever asked them for a penny; there is none, in the whole of England, who can say that I ever asked them for a penny; there is none under heaven, in the whole wide world, who can say that I ever asked them for a penny. To God, and to God alone, I went; and I did this because I knew ever since my conversion that one of the greatest necessities for the Church of God at large was an increase of faith. Therefore, I determined to dedicate my whole life to this one great lesson, for the Church of God to learn, and the world at large to learn: real, true, lasting dependence on God.

Thus I have now been going on for 68 years, not only regarding the work of God, but regarding my own temporal necessities and the necessities of my family, and I have laid every burden on God, and God again and again has helped me. He has also led me to the founding of many schools. I have had 117 schools under my direction throughout England, Scotland, India, the Straits of Malacca, British Guiana, Demerara, Essequibo, Berlice, in Spain, in France, in Italy, and in other parts of the world. And in these schools have been educated 122,000 young people. One hundred and twenty-two thousand young people; and from among them, more than 20,000 have been converted that we know of. In heaven I expect to meet more than 40,000 or 50,000; but we know that more than 20,000 were converted while they were in the schools, the masters having given reports. Sometimes fifty and sixty in half-a-year in one single school have been brought to the knowledge of the Lord, and thus has it gone on that God has abundantly blessed the work.

Then, in regard to the circulation of the Holy Scriptures, God has abundantly blessed that. Bibles in various languages to the number of 279,000 I have been enabled to circulate, and 1440,000 New Testaments, 21,000 copies of the Book of Psalms, and 222,000 other portions; and God has also abundantly blessed this part of the work, especially in Spain, in Italy, and in Ireland. Then as to missionary operations, I have been enabled to aid a large number of missionaries and helpers, and altogether I have spent £258,000 on missions alone. The matter of the circulation of tracts was also particularly laid on my heart, and God has granted me the privilege of circulating 109 millions of Scriptural books, pamphlets, and tracts-not 109 thousand, but a thousand times as much. One hundred and nine millions of books, pamphlets, and tracts, in various languages-so many that this large hall would not hold them, and 400 big cart horses would not be able to drag them away! To such an extent have tracts and books been circulated.

Thousands of souls have been brought to Jesus through the instrumentality of the four or five hundred missionaries that I have sought to assist, and as for the Orphan work, I have been enabled to receive 9,750 orphans. That may seem to you a small number in comparison with what we can have at one time in the houses. The reason is this: we have the orphan girls and boys from their earliest days, and often and often we have girls in the houses fifteen years, sixteen years, even seventeen years, and in a few instances longer than seventeen years. That is the reason why the number has been comparatively so small, though we have the accommodation of the greatest Orphan institution under heaven. There is not a second Orphan "institution in the whole wide world so large as that on Ashley Down. Out of these 9,750 orphans, between 4,000 and 5,000 have been brought to the knowledge of Jesus; more than 2,000 are already in heaven; over 2,000 are walking in various parts of the world as believers, and we have at present about 000 in the Orphan houses who are believers.

One single point more for your encouragement, and for the sake that my beloved Christian friends may be led increasingly to give themselves to prayer, especially for the conversion of sinners. When I came to Bristol, sixty-four years and seven months since, and we met for the first time in the breaking of bread at the Lord's Supper, there were seven of us. That was all "Seven of us." Since then there have been received by us, as a Church, more than 6,000 into fellowship. Let this be another encouragement to go forward. And when the branch Churches that have sprung out of the Church at Bethesda are taken in, O how many thousands more! So let this be a great encouragement for prayer. Seven, meeting the first time round the Lord's table! And now look at the many, many thousands who have been converted since, and been received at the Lord's table.

Are there any here who have not yet believed? See what God is willing to give in answer to prayer. See what He is willing to give to you, my dear young man, my dear young woman, and you elder friends. If any of you do not know the Lord, see what God is willing to do in answer to prayer. I am a poor, miserable sinner myself, deserving nothing but hell if I had my deserts; but see what God has given to a poor miserable sinner, simply for Christ's sake. I trust in Him, and therefore, for Christ's sake, He has given to me; and what He has given to me, He is willing to give to you. O expect blessings from Him, and He will give them to you, if you seek them by earnest prayer.

For instance, are any weak and feeble as to the body, suffering pain, or needing anything in reference to their health. This text applies to then, "Open thy mouth wide, and I will fill it." The very connection in which this stands here in this verse gives to us the assurance that we shall have blessing in God's own time and way, for it was He Who brought, under the most difficult circumstances, the Israelites out of Egypt. Neither Pharoah nor his servants would let them go; he had kept them long as slaves, made them to work continually under the most trying circumstances. Everything that the Scripture tells us was done to them was done with rig our, whether they were brick-makers, or were working in the fields, or were building stone cities for Pharoah. Nothing in that treatment escaped. Jehovah says, through Moses and Aaron, to Pharoah, "Let them go." The reply of Pharoah is against Jehovah, " I know not Jehovah; I do not mean to let them go." Presently, when this request is repeated and neglected, and there comes a judgment on him, he minds it not. There comes one judgment after the other, and one judgment after the other increases more and more; but he will not let them go. At last comes the most awful of all the judgments; in every house throughout the country one is taken, the firstborn throughout the land slain in one night by the destroying angel who goes through the land. Now the Israelites are allowed to go; yea, driven out of the country for fear they should all be dead men if they were not to let them go.

Thus we see what God is able to do in man's behalf, seeing that He, under these circumstances, could get out of the state of bondage and slavery those hundreds of thousands of Israelites. And not merely is the power of Jehovah seen in this verse, but His love also. Who were these Israelites? Were they better than the Egyptians? They were decidedly worse than the Egyptians, because they had more knowledge than the Egyptians, and yet were a stiff-necked, rebellious, hard, wicked people. But notwithstanding all this, Jehovah brings them out of the country by reason of the love He has for them, and by reason of the covenant into which He had entered with Abraham, Isaac, and Jacob, and because He is Jehovah, the covenant-keeping God. Now in all this can we not see especial encouragement in regard to our own case? If, therefore, we need anything in reference to our bodies, let us go to our Heavenly Father. Do we need anything in reference to our family positions? Tried by our children, tried, greatly tried it may be, by the husband or wife, or perhaps by our relatives? Let us bring these things before God! It is no use complaining, speaking about it particularly to one another; no, instead of murmuring, bring this matter often before God in prayer, look to Him for help and support, and entreat Him again and again that He would, in the riches of His grace, deliver you out of your trials.

Then again, in reference to our business, our earthly occupation, our profession. Axe there particular trials? Are there particular difficulties? Instead of continually talking and fretting about the competition, the difficult times, the tricks manifested in trades and businesses, the matter should be carried to the Lord. Meekly, quietly, gently, submissively behaving ourselves under the circumstances, and again, again, and again bringing the matter before God and leaving it there. And we should find that this is the very best remedy which could be used! Then not merely in reference to temporal matters, but to spiritual things also, this is to be applied. For instance, in our spiritual conflict there is nothing better than to remember this gracious, this most precious promise, "Open thy mouth wide, and I will fill it." We feel the natural evil tendencies within us, we struggle against them, we seek to overcome them, we find ourselves too weak, but God is able to help us, and out of these things He will bring us. Our text says, "Open thy mouth wide, and I will fill it," and so it encourages us to come to God and ask great blessings in respect to these things, and we shall find how ready He is to help us so that pride and high-mindedness, carelessness and slothfulness, indulgence in natural evil tendencies, can be overcome by the power of God the Holy Spirit.

Then in reference to our work and labour and service for the Lord, as Sunday School teachers, as tract distributors, as visitors of the sick. In all these matters we can obtain help from God. In ourselves extremely weak, let us seek help in the right way. As teachers it: the Church of God, as pastors, as labourers in any way spiritually, wonderful help can be obtained from God in answer to prayer, so that if we "open our mouths wide" we shall find the text fulfilled.

The second point in connection with this is especially to be noticed. "He will fill it." "Open thy mouth wide, and I will fill it." "I will fill it." "I will fill it." It is not stated, "Perhaps I will fill it," or "I shall see if I will do it or not." No promise of this kind. He does not say, "If thou art doing so and so, I will fill it." We have not to fill our mouth after we have opened it wide; that is, we have not by our own power and ability and skilfulness to bring about the fulfilment of the promise. We have to leave this to God. He will do it. We have not to look to our fellow-men to bring about the answer to prayer, as often is the case on the part of dear children of God. They look to their fellow-men, instead of having the eye fixed upon the almighty power of God and the loving heart of God; they look to their fellowmen to answer their prayers. "I will fill it," He says. We have not to look to circumstances, or to a contingency in everyday things and affairs, but to God Himself is the eye to be directed. "I will fill it." "I will fill it."

Then, in the third place, we have not to be discouraged because our mouth is not at once filled; we have not to be discouraged because the answer does not come immediately. Beloved brethren and sisters in Christ, ever be mindful of the fact that in connection with all the many hundreds of promises given to us in connection with prayer, in the Old and New Testaments of the Holy Scriptures, there is not one single passage to be found where God makes in connection with this promise a statement regarding the time when He will fulfil it. He simply states everywhere, "I will do it," "I will answer it." He never says, "At such a time I will answer," " At such a time I will fill your mouth. But He simply states "I will do it." And often and often the delay is found appointed by God so that when the answer comes it may be all the more lovely to us and more suitable to us than if the answer had been immediately given. Yes, and another reason, in order that by the exercise of faith and patience, faith and patience may develop further and further, and increase more and more. There is another, a third, reason. That we may by the exercise of faith and patience glorify God. The world looks on to see how shall we behave ourselves under especial trials and difficulties, what we shall do. Now, if they find us waiting without fretting, without complaining, and especially without murmuring, then they may perceive that we are looking after the things of God, and this may lead to blessing too. Thus by such behaviour we strengthen the hands of our fellow-men.

And then often and often in the experience of the children of God answers to prayer are delayed because their hearts are not yet prepared for the reception of the blessing. I will give you an illustration. Suppose there is a young convert going to work in the Sunday School; he has heard a great deal about answers to prayer, and he longs for answers to prayer, and begins to pray that it may please God very speedily to convert all the children in his class. He goes the first Sunday; he does not find that they are all converted. He goes the second Sunday, the third, and the fourth Sunday, and it is not accomplished. He is tried now, and becomes distressed. He says to himself, "pray so much that all the children under my care in the class may be converted, and yet I go Sunday after Sunday, and they remain unconverted. How comes this?" The reason is because this dear brother is not yet prepared for receiving the blessing, for if the class so very easily were brought to the knowledge of the Lord Jesus Christ, he would take the credit to himself, and begin to look upon himself and to 'say what an excellent teacher he is, and how much he could accomplish in the conversion of those scholars, instead of its all being' done by the power at the Holy Ghost. The heart is not yet prepared for the reception of the blessing; therefore the blessing is delayed. But let this beloved young brother go on waiting upon God, coming more and more to see that he can do nothing in the way of converting sinners, that all must be accomplished by the power of the Holy Ghost, then when the blessing is given, and the class converted, he will be prepared to give all the honour and glory to God.

Thus often and often we find that the hindrance to the answer to prayer lies in ourselves, because our hearts are not yet prepared for a blessing.

Chapter 17: Christ, the Refuge of Sinners!

A Sermon preached at Kensington Baptist Chapel, Stapleton Road, Bristol, on Sunday morning, March 28th, 1897, on the occasion of the Chapel Anniversary.

1 Tim. 1:15.

IN THE FIRST part of this statement-"Christ Jesus came into the world to save sinners " - it is recorded that it is a "faithful saying" - not a questionable saying, or one that is exposed to the shadow of a doubt! We, who are believers in the Lord Jesus Christ, should make it habitually our business to show by our life and love for God that we believe implicitly in the truth of the statement that Jesus Christ came into the world to save sinners! Therefore, our business is to be faithful witnesses for the truth of the Gospel!

It is next stated that "it is worthy of all acceptation." It is worthy, therefore, to be received by us; it is our duty to receive this statement that Christ Jesus came into the world to save sinners. Now what do we say regarding this? Do we individually all of us set our seal to this by receiving it implicitly? There are very many here at present who do so. I question not that there are hundreds here present who do so-who have received this statement of God's Holy Spirit that Christ Jesus came into the world to save sinners! But my heart's desire and prayer is that everyone of you, without exception, may receive this statement. There is no other Saviour but Jesus Christ, and we must receive this truth into our hearts. There is no other way regarding the salvation of our souls but through Him! O let us lay this to heart!

And then we have to consider that "He came into the world," not that He was born into the world! This is particularly to be noticed. If it had been stated that He was born into the world, it would have been true so far as regards his human nature. Mary was His mother according to His human nature; but the divinity of our Lord Jesus is referred to here. Our Saviour was really and truly a man as much as we are; but He was really and truly God as God the Father. It would have been quite true if it had been stated that He was born into the world to save sinners. But here, however, the divinity of our Lord is pointed out to us! He is the Creator of everything that exists; the Builder, the Upholder, of everything that exists. But as the divinity of our blessed Lord is here referred to, it was necessary that He should be really and truly divine as the Father of our souls! That He should be human was necessary in order that, in our form and state, he might fulfil the law of God which we have broken times without number, and thus work out the righteousness in which we can now find ourselves, but which by nature we cannot of ourselves obtain, for we have nothing of our own. Of our own righteousness we cannot be accepted by God! In the Word of God it is compared to filthy rags. By God's love, the righteousness of Christ is imputed to all those who trust in Him for salvation; and solely on the ground of the righteousness of Christ, poor sinners-old and young-male and female-rich and poor-educated or uneducated-any and everyone trusting alone in the Lord Jesus Christ for salvation shall be accepted!

Now, it was necessary that he should be human in order that, as a human being, born under the law, he should fulfil the law of God which we have broken times without number, by action, by word, by thought, by feeling, by desire, by purpose, and by inclination! But the righteousness of Christ shall be put to our account-shall be reckoned to our account! We shall ourselves be considered as if we had fulfilled the law of God, if we put our trust in Christ!

Further, it was necessary that He should be really and truly human in order that our sin might be punished in the person of the substitute-that punishment might actually be borne by the person who was to be our substitute--even the Man Christ Jesus! And therefore the substitute, in order to make a real atonement for our sins; must bear this punishment in our room and stead.

But this is only one side of the truth. The other side of the truth is this: He was truly divine as the Father; and it was necessary to give value to the righteousness entrusted to Him and imputed to us, and also to give value to the atonement, that the Lord Jesus Christ Himself hung upon the cross and shed His blood for the remission of our sins! A mere human being might have been crucified; but this human being would merely have been punished himself through the death of crucifixion. This, however, would not have given value to the blood that was shed. It must be the blood of the God-man, Christ Jesus! This very blood which was shed is called the "blood of God" -for He was truly God as well as man-was shed for the remission of our sins; and it was just this which gave the value to the blood, for it was to be efficacious in the salvation not merely of one sinner, nor a thousand, nor a million poor sin-sick souls; but an innumerable company were to be saved by this blood-the blood of that blessed Jesus who took our sins-my sins, your sins-upon Him. Therefore the blood, to be of value, must be the blood of the God-man, Christ Jesus! This is the valuable part-the all-important fact to be remembered by us!-Christ's blood can save us from all sin! And we can only be saved through Him who shed His precious blood for our ransom and regeneration!

And now, my dear friends, how precious is this thought! Yes, how precious! The law has been fulfilled! I am a poor, wicked, hell-deserving sinner-you, and I, too, are poor miserable sinners under the law; yet, if you put your trust in the Lord Jesus Christ, God will accept and receive you through the righteousness of Christ which is put to your credit, reckoned to your account, imputed to you!

The Lord Jesus Christ has made an atonement for every one of our numberless transgressions, for all our sinful ways, sinful words, wicked thoughts! That blessed, precious, adorable, loving Saviour has made an atonement for every one of our sinful words as well as sinful actions! Yes! He has made an atonement! And not only was this atonement to be for every one of our sinful thoughts, unholy desires, ungodly wishes and inclinations, but the Lord Jesus Christ made the atonement to the full! And thus it comes that the poor sinner is saved! O how precious! How comforting to our sin-sick souls!

Now, the next point that we have especially to consider is this: He came into the world to save SINNERS! Yes, my dear friends, sinners! It does not say that He came into the world to save EXCELLENT people, or those who are very good, or those who are only moderate sinners! Then I must go to hell, for I was a great sinner for the first twenty years of my life. For several years I was pursuing the pleasures of the world-the vanities of the world-the vices of the world! These were what I followed! And yet I went to the University to study for a clergyman! Yes! that was the intention-to make me a clergyman. I attended the Classical Schools; and for nine years after I entered the University, and attended the examinations to become a clergyman-I say for nine years, from the time that I was ten and a half till I was nineteen and a half-and still preparing for a clergyman, I was living far from God! For six years-from the time that I was fourteen till I was twenty years of age-I never read one single chapter of the Bible-not one single verse! I read the Hebrew and the Greek New Testament, and had the Bible in my own language, but I never read it!

This was the state in which God found me! There was nothing for me but hell I-nothing but hell! I knew nothing of that wondrous cross until God opened my eyes, when I was twenty years and five months old, and showed me what a wicked young man I was, and that I was deserving of nothing but hell! But, blessed be His Name, he also showed me from this precious Book that even such a wicked, hell-deserving sinner as I was could be saved from my sins through the blood of Christ and through the atonement which had been made for poor sinners!

Now, I had not your privileges. I had never in my early life heard the Gospel till I was twenty years and five months of age! I had never heard of a real true Christian in my life! No doubt there were many; but I had never heard or seen one! And yet I was one of a number of students in the University who were preparing to become clergymen!

About this time I was led to a little prayer meeting which was held in the house of a tradesman. There were about a dozen or fifteen citizens in the room; and here I, for the first time, heard of Christ. I entered the house of this tradesman as dead in trespasses and sins, and as utterly reckless and careless of divine things as any person in existence. I came away from that little prayer meeting a happy young man-a happy believer in Christ! There were at this time twelve hundred and sixty students in the University; but only three of them were believers in Christ, and I became the fourth! This was the state of things in which I was found when I attended that little prayer meeting, and where for the first time I heard the name of Jesus! Merry company-worldly company-was all that I cared about. I met with nothing but disappointment. Instead of finding happiness in these things, I met with nothing but disappointment.

At last I thought I would travel a great deal and find if that would make me happier. God led me. I travelled for forty-three days in succession-day by day for forty-three days j and I saw some of the most beautiful scenery that is to be found under the canopy of heaven. After the lapse of several weeks, I became so sick and tired and surfeited with travelling that I could pass the most beautiful scenery without looking at it.

But three weeks after I had found Jesus in this little prayer meeting I became a truly happy man; and I have had true, real happiness now for seventy-one years and five months!

This real, true happiness, my friends, I desire for everyone of you who is without it; and it is for that reason that I am standing here this morning to bear witness for the Lord Jesus Christ! How many of you have this real, true happiness which I have found in the Lord Jesus Christ?

When I carne home from that little prayer meeting --now more than seventy years ago--l found myself lying peacefully on my bed blessing and praising God for what He had been doing for me! No believer I conversed with; no one said to me, "Now, mind! you must give up the card-table, and the theatre, and the ball-room, and all those evil ways in which you have been going on." No! but God had given me spiritual life-spiritual instincts-spiritual desires. But I said to myself on that first evening after I carne from that little prayer meeting, "I shall never go any more to the ball-room, or play cards." And I have never been to the ball-room or played cards since. The whole life became different. All at once it became different, because now I was no longer dead in trespasses and in sins. I had now obtained spiritual life, and joyfully and gladly surrendered myself to God, Who had done so much, so very much, for me. And thus I became unspeakably happy.

And I have, my dear friends, been most unspeakably happy ever since, which is now for seventy-one years and five months.

O what a glorious idea-how simple!-how precious!-that through the Gospel of glad tidings preached to us, and coming to, and trusting alone m Jesus, sinners-great sinners, old sinners-may be saved!

After the Apostle had been making this statement that "Christ Jesus came into the world to save sinners," he says "Of whom I am chief!" This is not a mere formal expression; it is what St. Paul meant; he considered himself a very great sinner-the greatest sinner: and Paul called himself the chief of sinners! This is not the only passage in which he refers to himself; but, again and again, in his Epistles and in the Acts of the Apostles, he speaks of himself as a very great sinner.

Then comes the next verse which follows the text: "Howbeit for this cause I obtained mercy, that in me first Jesus Christ might show forth all long-suffering, for a pattern to them which should hereafter believe on Him to life everlasting."

I am now ninety-one years and six months of age, with the prospect of heaven-very near heaven-very near the end of my earthly pilgrimage! Still I am able to work every day, and all the day long. I preach five or six times a week besides; and am able to do it! But although in my ninety-second year, speaking after the manner of men, there is the prospect of being taken away, yet I am unspeakably happy!

And it is unspeakably happy to be able to help one another trusting in Jesus! Never forget that Jesus came to save sinners-such a sinner as I was! But you must accept salvation in God's appointed way. It is through Jesus alone that you can be saved! If sinners in their own way seek to bring themselves to heaven, they will bring themselves to hell! hell! HELL! Yes, they will bring themselves to hell by their good works--by their own righteousness! Sinners can be alone saved by trusting in Jesus for salvation, for He is Lord!

That is, that the Lord Jesus Christ, in showing to Paul-formerly named Saul, the great persecutor-that as the Lord had saved Paul, a great sinner as He was, so our Saviour thereby showed to every sinner under heaven at any time afterwards that no one need despair of the possibility of obtaining forgiveness! This is a most vital and precious truth! "For this cause I obtained mercy!" That means, "I have obtained forgiveness, for this very cause that, in me, the greatest sinner, the chief of sinners. Jesus Christ might show those "all long-suffering.'" That means, "How much He is now suffering, because what He is ready to do for sinners is not immediately and completely taken advantage of." That certainly does not mean such as are not particularly great sinners. But that He is willing to forgive the greatest sinner. Paul was willing to become a sample-a pattern-so that not a single individual hereafter might have ground for saying, "I am too hardened a sinner! I have lived too long in sin! My sins are too great and too many to bear! I cannot expect forgiveness!" Nothing of the kind! Paul is here given as a sample-a pattern-a specimen-of what God is willing to forgive, and what the Lord Jesus Christ is willing to do in regard to any and every sinner. But that is by "simply trusting in Him" Who has paid the penalty of sin for us by the shedding of His own blood.

O, my friends, how precious! Yes, how precious! Perhaps there is one here present who says, "My mother has wept over me-begged me, with many a tear running down her aged cheeks, to alter my course and become different; but I am a wretched, guilty sinner, and have continued in my sin up to now!" Ah, my friends! Guilty as you may be-though you could stand against the tears of your poor, dear, aged mother, who has wept over you times out of number-yet even you shall be forgiven if you seek for forgiveness through the righteousness and love of the Lord Jesus Christ!

O how precious! Yes, how precious! Saul was forgiven in order that not a single individual under heaven might say, "I am too old-too great a sinner-too hardened-my sins are too many." Nothing of the kind! If you only seek salvation through Jesus Christ, you may obtain mercy. How unspeakably precious!

This brings before us the point that whilst yet in the body we may know that we are forgiven sinners. We may know that God has forgiven us, and reconciled us to Himself. Do all here present enjoy this know ledge of the forgiveness of their sins? This is what I desire regarding every one here. I have not the shadow of a doubt that there are a vast number here present who do know and enjoy the knowledge of the forgiveness of their sins. But do you all? I have enjoyed the knowledge of the forgiveness of my sins. I have not the least doubt I am as certain that I shall go to heaven as if I were there already. But I deserve nothing but hell. I am a believer, however; and the Word of God declares that God so loved the world that He spared not His own Son, but gave Him up for us, so that every believer in Him should have everlasting life-that we might go to heaven. Now, I do believe in Him. Therefore it is certain that I shall be in heaven. The Word of God declares concerning the Lord Jesus that He is the Saviour of sinners; that all who believe and trust in Him for salvation shall obtain the remission of their sins-that is, the forgiveness of their sins. The 43rd verse of the 10th chapter of the Acts of the Apostles states this emphatically: "To Him give all the prophets witness, that through His Name whosoever believeth in Him shall receive remission of sins. Therefore I know that my sins will be forgiven through faith in Christ; and that I shall go to heaven if I trust in the Lord Jesus!

Then, again, we may know that our sins are forgiven even whilst we are here. It is not a matter of indifference to us whether we know it or no. It is of vast importance to us that we should have knowledge of this fact even here, for there is no real state of enjoyment in God without knowing that we are accepted in Him-that our sins are blotted out by the atonement which the Lord Jesus has made for us!

And now, my dear friends, I would therefore affectionately press this point upon every one of you who are believers in Christ. If you have not the knowledge that your sins are forgiven, I would earnestly and lovingly entreat you to give yourselves no rest until you know Christ; and if you trust in Christ alone for salvation, then, according to the passage which I have just quoted, it is certain that your sins are forgiven. Therefore, we may have peace in God, and thus be strong in the Lord, for the joy of the Lord is our strength in the proportion in which we are working for, and loving and trusting in, God. We are dead to the world, and to all its evil influences, if we are thoroughly trusting in Him!

O, my dear friends, it is of the utmost importance to us to know that we are forgiven, to know that we have obtained mercy. What says the' Apostle? " Howbeit for this cause I obtained mercy, that in me first "-in ME, such a great sinner, the Lord Jesus might make a beginning-to show, first, the vastness of his long-suffering-the degree of his long-suffering-the extent of his patience--for all those who should hereafter believe in Him. O! what a comforting thought to a poor heavy-laden sinner! No poor sinner now need despair of salvation-of being forgiven! What a precious thought! O so precious!

Then one word more. Life everlasting! Yes! Life everlasting! An eternity of happiness! A participation in the rivers of pleasure at the right hand of God! Having been washed in the blood of Christ, we are no longer dead in trespasses and sins. We are purified from sin-spiritualized! And O, what a glorious thought: that this spiritual life in us through the gift of the Holy Ghost is everlasting! It is not fully developed yet! It will be fully developed when the Lord takes us to Himself-fully developed through the praise and honour and glory of God! O how precious is this blessing! Everyone here present this morning may obtain it! Here is a specimen before you of a guilty image-forgiven, and made a happy man! I have had this happiness now for seventy-one years and five months! And what God did for me, He is willing and ready to do for any and everyone who will accept Christ. O accept Him now!

I have travelled in forty-two countries in my missionary labours; but I think I may say that of the many millions of human beings with whom I came into contact who were deserving of hell, none of them were so deserving of hell as myself-the greatest sinner! This being so, I can assure you the only way to find acceptance in Christ is to trust in Him for full, complete forgiveness all your life! To everyone of you who has not obtained these blessings of which I have been speaking, I have come here this morning as a witness for Christ, for what the blessed Lord did for me He is as willing to do for you. Trust Him; and I am sure you will be happy. Amen.

Chapter 18: The Glad Tidings

A Sermon preached at Bethesda Chapel, Great George Street, Bristol, on April 18th, 1897.

1 Corinthians 15:1-3.

AMONG ALL THE other things that were wrong already in the days of the Apostles in the church at Corinth was this also: there were some there of the synagogue of Satan. Some among them disbelieved the resurrection of the body, and on this point the Apostle Paul writes, throughout the 15th chapter, and gives unto us most precious instruction regarding the resurrection.

The great point in the whole chapter in particular is this-if there be no resurrection, then the Lord Jesus Christ Himself has not been raised; if there be no resurrection, and Jesus Christ Himself has not been raised, on this account we are yet in our sins, we have not forgiveness, for there would be no such thing as proof of forgiveness had the Lord Jesus Christ not been raised from the dead. Moreover, if the Lord Jesus Christ was not raised from the dead, then I (the Apostle Paul) and my fellow-labourers are false witnesses of God, for we have testified that there is a resurrection, and that Christ was raised from the dead, when, after all, He was not raised; wherefore, the whole Gospel is no longer a Gospel. Now for this was this 15th chapter written, in which there is most precious instruction found connected with the resurrection.

"Moreover, brethren, I declare unto you the Gospel which I preached unto you." Remark here the word "brethren," "believers in Him." Naturally looking at it, we might say "this is just in an ordinary way; no stress is to be laid on it." My own judgment is the reverse. He calls them still "brethren," and he treats them still as brethren, though they had fallen into such errors as these, and failed as to their life and deportment in various ways. Yet he calls them still "Brethren," because he hoped that by the means he was going to employ, in writing another Epistle, they would be brought out of that state. And we find how greatly this letter was blessed when we read the second epistle to the church at Corinth. Thus we have to imitate the Apostle, and on no account, because we see the manifestations of weakness, in one shape or another, on the part of the children of God, to at once put them aside and disown them as believers, as if there were no grace at all in them. For, like the Corinthians, they may come out of that state, and they may yet greatly glorify God.

"I declare unto you the Gospel," that is, the glad tidings, the most precious glad tidings. The sum and substance of this we find in the third and fourth verses, where he says: "I delivered unto you first of all that which I also received, how that Christ died for our sins according to the Scriptures; and that He was buried, and that He rose again the third day according to the Scriptures." He died for our sins, to make an atonement for our sins, to bear the punishment in our room and stead; and that is the great point of what is called "The Gospel," "The Glad Tidings." The Gospel does not consist in this, that someone has left to us an exceedingly large amount of property, either in the way of money or in the way of estates; or that we shall now obtain a most lucrative position and employment; or that we shall be elevated to exceeding high rank or power. That is not the Gospel. These are not the glad tidings we have to ponder. But that, wicked hell-deserving sinners though we are, God in the riches of His Grace will forgive all our numberless transgressions; God, on the ground of the atonement of the Lord Jesus Christ, will forgive every one of our numberless transgressions, and not one single sin shall remain standing against us and do us any harm hereafter, because the Lord Jesus Christ has not merely for a thousand of our sins died and made atonement, nor merely for ten thousand of our sins, but for every one of the sins of which we have been guilty, however many they were, however great they were; nay, in whatever variety of ways we sinned, every one of our sins has been atoned for. O what good news is this! For were there one single sin remaining standing against us, we should be shut out thereby from the presence of God, for nothing that is defiled can enter into that presence. We must be spotless, pure; perfectly spotless and perfectly pure, else we cannot be where God is; and into this state we are brought through the righteousness of Christ, which is imputed to us through the atoning death of the Lord Jesus Christ, which removes every one of our numberless transgressions.

This, if rightly understood, if rightly entered into and apprehended, is what is called in the New Testament "The Gospel"; and we have to ask ourselves, "Is this our Gospel?" Do we trust in the Gospel? Or do we think that we must do our part, and that the Lord Jesus Christ will do His part? That we must do our part, else we cannot be saved? Nay, we must come to this, that we ourselves can do nothing; that everything was DONE by the Lord Jesus; that before He expired on the cross He exclaimed, "It is finished"-that is, everything that had to be done in the way of atonement had been accomplished by Him, and then, after He had uttered these words, He expired. This is the Gospel! Not doing one half of it, or one-eighth part of it, on our part to help the Lord Jesus Christ, so to speak! Nothing of the kind. He did everything, and except He had done everything most assuredly we must have perished.

Now of this Gospel the Apostle Paul says, "which I preached unto you." He was labouring at Corinth a year and six months (Acts xviii, 11.), and therefore again and again and again he had proclaimed these very truths, and those also of the resurrection of the Lord Jesus, and the resurrection of the believer; because without the resurrection there is no such thing as " the glad tidings" connected with Christ. That is the first point we have to notice. Now the second point of the Gospel is this, "Which also ye have received." Now here occurs a deeply important question, whether we have verily received these glad tidings, whether we verily rest the salvation of our souls on these glad tidings? As assuredly as we think that we have to do something ourselves for the salvation of our souls, and that the Lord Jesus Christ has not done everything that was necessary for our salvation, so assuredly are we yet in a most fatal mistake on earth.

We must come to this: that in our inmost soul we believe that Jesus Christ did everything which was necessary to make an atonement for our numberless, manifold transgressions, and that we have to do nothing but to stand in the position of beggars to receive what God gives us in Christ. And whosoever will not receive, as a poor worthless worm and as a beggar, what God gives to him, in Christ, such a one has not yet come to the state of heart that he might come to, and to which he ought to come, to have the full blessing of the Gospel. We have just to stand before God, simply receiving what He freely, in the way of grace, gives to us m Christ Jesus. We have done nothing, we are unable to do anything now, and we shall never be able hereafter to do the smallest particle, towards our salvation. Jesus did it all. Jesus finished all that was necessary to be done for the salvation of our souls.

Now, then, to receive the Gospel means in other words that we have to own that we are sinners; we have to own in prayer before God that we deserve nothing but punishment for our sins, and that we can do nothing whatever towards the salvation of our souls; but that the Lord Jesus Christ has accomplished everything that was needful to be accomplished, and that we gratefully accept what God gives us in Christ. This is to receive the Gospel. Now I affectionately ask my dear Christian friends, Have we thus received the Gospel? Is this that to which we look for the salvation of our souls. You know we must own before God that we are sinners; we must confess before God in prayer that we are sinners, and simply and entirely for our salvation put our trust in Jesus, and nothing else; and in doing this we receive the Gospel, but if otherwise we have not yet received the Word.' This is the second point.

Then in the third place, the Apostle says, "Wherein ye stand." What does it mean to stand in the Gospel? It means that regarding ourselves and the Lord Jesus Christ we maintain still that we are just in such a state as we were before, and can do nothing concerning the salvation of our souls. In other words, that after ten years of conversion, or twenty years, or fifty years, and the seeking to hate sin more and more, and to love holiness more and more, we maintain still, and will maintain to the end of our life, that we are sinners; that we deserve nothing but punishment; that we cannot save ourselves, or do anything in the least for ourselves in the matter of salvation; that we depend still, as we did at the first, entirely on what the Lord Jesus Christ did and suffered in our room and stead. If this is the mind in which we are, then we stand in the Gospel; if not, we do not stand in the Gospel. We must till the end of our earthly pilgrimage remain of the same mind in which we were when first we came to Christ. Each must own, "I am a sinner; I deserve nothing but punishment. If I am saved, it must be in the way of grace, through a Substitute, Who in my room and stead fulfilled the law which I had broken times without number, and Who in my room, as Substitute, bore the punishment due to me."

If this is the state of our heart and mind, then we are standing in the Gospel; if it is otherwise, if in the least degree we take the smallest particle of credit to ourselves in the matter of salvation, we are not standing in the Gospel. A deeply important point! And it is particularly for another reason important that we have this mind. Important not merely regarding the final salvation, but regarding the present peace and joy in God, for he or she taking the least particle of credit to himself or herself in the matter of salvation loses the peace of God and real, true spiritual enjoyment, for God is determined to give all the honour and glory to His Only-begotten Son-the choicest Gift He had to bestow on poor sinners. And He will not, therefore, with a sinful human creature divide the glory of what belongs to Christ, and to Christ alone.

Now the last point. "By which also"-that is, by the Gospel-" by which also ye are saved, if ye keep in memory what I preached unto you, unless ye have believed in vain." By the Gospel we are saved! Precious! O delightful news. Because it is such good news, therefore it is called the Gospel. The Gospel means "glad tidings," "good news"; and these are the glad tidings: that we are at last saved by the Gospel. In the first place, salvation consists in this-that we get a glorified body, completely free, and free for eternity from all weakness, weariness, pain, suffering, langour, sickness of any kind, and from death. No longer exposed to death. Now how pleasant is the news of this!

Then, again, as to weariness, irrespective of suffering. Children of God delight to labour for the Lord; it is an exceeding great joy to them to work six, or eight hours, in the course of the day, and some by reason of health and strength are delighted to spend ten and twelve hours in working for the Lord, and some surpass even this; but yet, however long we may be able to work while in the body here on earth, though it be sixteen or even eighteen hours, at last most assuredly there will come the weariness, the weakness, the inability to go on working any longer. But when we obtain our glorified body, when salvation comes to the full, no more of this weariness.

Yea, there will be the working four and twenty hours, day by day, throughout the whole week, seven times four and twenty hours (speaking after the manner of men) without the least weariness; and thus it will go on throughout the whole months, and throughout the whole years (speaking after the manner of men), and not a particle of weakness or weariness experienced while thus engaged for the Lord. And so it will be year after year, and one ten years after the other ten years, and one hundred years after the other hundred years, and one thousand years after the other thousand years, and never a particle of weakness or weariness experienced, when once salvation is completed and we obtain our glorious body. O how delightful is this! What glad tidings are these! And if they were held on to by faith, the heart would be full, brimful of joy!

O how delightful we should be if really and truly entering into all this; but there is something even more precious still-all this service will be joyfully rendered to the Lord, and be perfectly free from failure and shortcomings. There will not be a single particle of sin mixed up with our work and labour for the Lord. At present, while we are in the body, in this state of weakness and imperfection, with all our holy longing, with all our prayerful desire, yea, with our earnest prayers, still now and then is mingled a word which is not quite according to the mind of God; a thought which was not found in the blessed Jesus, and therefore not perfectly according to the mind of God.

But when brought to see Jesus as He is, and made like Him in body and soul, everything that we do will be perfectly Christ-like, everything that we say will be perfectly Christ-like; all that we think, that we desire, that we wish, for which we have inclination, all will be perfectly according to the mind of Christ. O what a blessed prospect is this for weak ones as we are, for erring ones as we are, for such who have their spiritual infirmities, great and many and varied, though hating sin and loving holiness. O what bright and glorious prospects are these! And all this is not merely a fancy of ours, but a reality.

We shall, verily, the weakest spiritually among us, be brought to this state of things when once salvation is complete! And this will never be altered, this will never be lost; we shall be throughout eternity in perfect, full, complete communion with the Lord Jesus Christ, and in fellowship habitually with Him-what commonly is called partnership; in complete, holy, godly partnership with Christ in every way! O how precious! Yea, in partnership with God the Father, not merely with the Lord Jesus Christ, our elder Brother. O how precious! How bright! How glorious are our prospects! And were all this known and entered into, everybody in the whole world would care about Christ; but because it is not known, and, if known, not believed, therefore the number of those who really and truly surrender the heart to. Christ is yet so small.

Now let us lay all these things to heart. Let us, if we have never yet treated them as realities, do so from this evening; from henceforth for the rest of our lives. There is one word more. "By which also ye are saved, if ye keep in memory what I preached unto you, unless ye have believed in vain." We must hold fast what was declared unto us by the Apostle; we have not to listen to false teachers, we have not to listen to those who pervert the Gospel, we have not to receive the statements of such teachers whereby the churches in the Roman province of Galatia were deluded in thinking that they must be circumcised and keep the law of God, like the Israelites did, in order to be saved. Nothing of the kind. Salvation is given to us in a way of grace, and through faith in Christ, through trusting in that which the Lord Jesus Christ has done and suffered. This is what the Apostle refers to. "If ye keep in memory what I preached unto you." Ye must hold fast the statements of the Apostles, "unless ye have believed in vain." The blessing will be lost, if we do not keep in memory the teaching of the Apostles.

Therefore, in the days in which we live, when good works are mixed up with the work of Christ, we have to be warned by all this; and, in childlike simplicity, enquire and go on enquiring what did Paul preach, what did Peter preach, what did John preach, and what did the other Apostles say. We have to find out this in the New Testament, and to hold fast to what they say. This is the way of continuing in the ways of God, and enjoying the truth of the Gospel; and therefore to be blessed with peace and joy in the Holy Ghost.

God grant this to all here present; and should there be one individual who is as yet looking to his or her doings for salvation, let him or her remember-I say it once more-we can alone be saved through Christ, and not anyone of us by our own doings.

Chapter 19: Spiritual Building.

A Sermon preached at Philip Street Baptist Chapel, Bedminster, Bristol, on Sunday Morning; Nov. 12th, 1893.

Jude, 20.

IN READING THIS short epistle of Jude, we learn that while yet one or other of the apostles was living, a great departure from the truth, and conformity to the mind of Christ, had already begun in the Church of God, and thus ever since, more or less, it has been; yea, and at certain times an awful darkness and great departure from the truth and godliness have been found in the Church of God, but, on the other hand, there have been also in the darkest days some truly godly ones, holding fast the truth as it is in Jesus, and seeking to tread in the footsteps of their Divine Master. Now, beloved in Christ, our holy, godly aim and purpose should be this, and our earnest prayer to God that we may be strengthened for this; that we belong to the little company holding fast the truths as to a crucified, risen, and ascended Saviour, and seeking more and more to be minded like Christ, dead to all that which is sinful and hateful to God in the world, and alive to all that pleases Him and is agreeable to His mind.

Our text shows to us how it should be with us. "But ye, beloved, building up yourselves on your most holy faith." It is on these words that I desire particularly to speak this morning. The figure used here we are all familiar with. It is taken from the erection of a building. According to the size of the building, whether it is high and large, so the foundation is laid- the foundation deep and broad, according to the size and height of the building.

Now, we all know what this signifies. The Apostle Paul tells us plainly no other foundation can be laid but Jesus Christ. What does this mean? That we cannot save ourselves, that our fellow-men cannot save us- that none but the Lord Jesus saves us, and can save us. Then how is this brought about? We have to own before God that we are sinners, and that we deserve nothing but punishment. We have to confess this openly before God, and then put our whole trust in the Lord Jesus Christ for the salvation of our souls-that is, trusting alone in the righteousness which He wrought out for poor sinners in fulfilling in their room and stead the law of God, which we had broken times without number, by our deeds, by our words, and by our thoughts, and put our whole trust in His perfect obedience unto death, the death of the cross, because when that Blessed One hung on the cross, when He shed His blood, it was for the remission of our sins. While He hung on the cross He made atonement for everyone of our sinful deeds, unholy words, ungodly thoughts, desires, purposes, and inclinations, and thus the wrath of God, the holiness of God, and the justice of God were satisfied. When He fulfilled the law, and stood in our room, He satisfied the holiness of God. When He bore the punishment while hanging on the cross in our room, He satisfied the justice of God, and every poor sinner trusting in Him alone for the salvation of the soul shall be forgiven. Before going on to our second part of the subject, I ask everyone of my beloved friends here present, "Have you ever been convinced that you are sinners needing a Saviour?" If not, ask God to have mercy on you, and to show you this. When you are convinced that you are sinners, have you confessed it before God? Have you humbled yourselves before God? Have you condemned yourselves, and passed sentence on yourselves before God? If not, ask God to help you to do so. But all this, while it is beginning in the right way, is not all.

The great point is to put our sole trust in Jesus Christ for salvation, for we can do nothing whatever in the matter of our salvation-the blessed Lord Jesus did it all. He finished the work for poor, guilty, hell-deserving sinners, as I am, and everyone of you are. The Lord Jesus fulfilled the law of God, and bore the punishment which that law demands should be inflicted on account of transgression. Either we must bear the punishment ourselves, or we must obtain a substitute. The blessed Lord Jesus voluntarily gave Himself to be our substitute, and if you put your trust in Him alone for salvation, God looks upon you as having fulfilled the law. This is the righteousness wrought out by the Lord Jesus, in our room and stead, for the greatest, the oldest, and the vilest of sinners, for if you put your trust in Him you have the substitute, Who, in your room, bore the punishment for you. How blessed to have a friend in Jesus! Do you enjoy the knowledge of the sweetness of this happiness? Without it, there is no lasting peace. The knowledge of forgiveness of sins is to be had while we are in the body. We are not to wait for it until the body is at an end. We can have it while we are alive. We should earnestly seek for it while we live. I have enjoyed for sixty-eight years the knowledge of the forgiveness of my sins, and, by the grace of God, I have not had a single minute's doubt whether my sins are forgiven or not; although a wretched, helpless sinner, all my sins are forgiven, and what God has done for me, a guilty, hell-deserving sinner, He is willing to do to everyone who seeks it in God's appointed way. Thus, owning we are sinners, and trusting in the Lord Jesus Christ for salvation, everyone who has done so is on the right foundation.

You all know that if a house is built, he who builds it does not simply lay the foundation, but there follows the superstructure, and adding stone to stone, and one piece of timber to another afterwards. Thus it is in the divine life. It is right to lay the proper foundation, but this is not all.

Almost all persons, after they are converted, are left here for a season. Comparatively few only are in the position of the dying thief-there was nothing in him but trust in the Lord Jesus. That was the foundation laid, and the Lord Jesus said, "Today shalt thou be with Me in paradise." But almost all persons, when they are brought to the knowledge of Jesus Christ, are left in the world for the purpose of becoming better acquainted with Him, and that they may see more of the vanity of this world, and the reality of heavenly things; and especially that they may bear fruit to the honour and glory of God, that they manifest the mind of Christ, that they seek to win souls to Christ, and do their part in helping the people of God both in spiritual and temporal things. For these reasons, being left here in the world, we have to seek to make progress in the divine life, and, as the text expresses it, "to build yourselves up on your most holy faith."

Before coming to this second part of our subject, I make one remark. You note it is "building up yourselves." Naturally, we should expect it to be said, "Let your pastors build you up; let your elders, let the deacons, let the aged, experienced Christians build you up on your most holy faith."

"Building up yourselves." The responsibility is laid upon every believer in the Lord Jesus Christ, that he do his part to make progress in the divine life.

Now, the great question before us is, "How is this to be done? How can we build up ourselves on our most holy faith?" Of all the Scriptures, the most blessed, precious answer to this question we find in 2 Peter i., to which we will now turn. "Simon Peter, a servant and an apostle of Jesus Christ, to them that have obtained like precious faith with us through the righteousness of God and our Saviour, Jesus Christ." Notice here, the apostles and every believer had the same kind of faith. The apostles had not one kind of faith, and other believers another kind of faith.

In the fifth verse we read, "And beside this, giving all diligence, add to your faith, virtue; and to virtue, knowledge" etc. Now, here we get the catalogue of what we have to do in these following verses-to build up ourselves in our most holy faith. If we have trust in Jesus Christ, faith in Him, the foundation is laid. Now, the next point at which we have to aim-and regarding which we have to cc give all diligence," not in a slothful way, but in "all diligence"-is to add to faith, virtue.

What have we to understand by this? The 4th chapter of Philippians, 8th verse, gives us the answer. "Finally, brethren, whatsoever things are true, whatsoever things are honest, whatsoever things are just, whatsoever things are pure, whatsoever things are lovely, whatsoever things are of good report; if there be any virtue, and if there be any praise, think on these things."

Here we see what is the first thing for any child of God, for any person brought to Jesus, where the right foundation has been laid regarding the salvation of the soul, is in order that he may be able to build up himself on his most holy faith, to aim at everything that is lovely, and bright, and pleasing in the sight of God, which implies that we avoid everything which is contrary to the mind of God-"if there be any virtue, and if there be any praise, think on these things." Now, as we are weak in ourselves, it becomes us to call upon God to help us to attain to this. To our "virtue" we are to seek to add "knowledge." The knowledge referred to here is not the knowledge of the things and affairs of this life. I do not despise knowledge concerning the ordinary things of this life, in reference to science or languages, which may be profitable to this fife, and may be useful and proper. While I allow this, it is not the kind of knowledge referred to here, but spiritual knowledge, the knowledge of the Lord Jesus, the knowledge of the vanity of this world, and of the reality of heavenly things; the knowledge which God has given to us in the Revelation which He has been pleased to make of Himself in the Holy Scriptures. It means, carefully to read the Scriptures, diligently to read the Scriptures, with prayer to read the Scriptures, and to meditate on the Word of God. Now let me ask my beloved brethren and sisters in Christ, Is this your habit? Are you habitually reading the Scriptures? There is great danger, through the multiplicity of matters, that we neglect the Word of God. There is great temptation lest through the multiplicity of books which are issued year after year from the press, we neglect the Holy Scriptures.

What will be the result of this? We shall injure ourselves spiritually, we shall not make progress in the divine life except we give ourselves carefully, habitually, diligently, and with meditation, to the reading of the Holy Scriptures. It is these means which God has specially used, and does use, for the advancement in divine life. Now as I love you, my beloved friends in Christ, and as I am come here for the purpose of leaving a blessing behind, with God's blessing, I affectionately ask you if you are lovers of the Word of God. Ask yourselves in the presence of God, "Am I a lover of the Word of God? "

For the first twenty years of my life I was not a lover of the Word of God. I neglected the Word of God. From the time when I was fourteen and a half years old until I was twenty years and five weeks old, I never read the Word of God. Then it pleased God to show me that I was a sinner, and needed a Saviour, and I saw how to put my trust in the Lord Jesus for salvation. Then I took to reading the Word of God, and I read it every day. I cannot say I was a real lover of the Word of God, but in July, 1829, four years after my conversion, I became a lover of the Word of God, and now for sixty-four years I have been a lover of the Word of God, and it is a great delight to me to have the Word of God. I cannot tell you what a blessing it is to my soul. Blessed as I have been for fifty-eight years with work, my habit is first of all to have a good meal for my soul. I come to the Word of God, I read it, I pray over it, I meditate on it, and I apply it to myself. How does this comfort you? how does it exhort you? how does it warn you?

how does it reprove you? Thus I read the Scriptures, and get a blessing to my soul, and then I go to work with all my might, with earnestness, but I do not go to my work until I first have a good meal for my soul. And what has been the consequence? I am a healthy man, day after day, week after week, month after month, year after year. I have now entered on my eighty-ninth year. I am not cold, and dull, and lifeless, spiritually; I am a healthy man, spiritually, and the great instrument that has been used by God for this is the Word of God, which I read with delight and joy, and which I would my beloved brethren and sisters in Christ do the same. They would find the healthfulness I have had, and the continued happiness I have had, year after year, and which I have now had for sixty-eight years. There is nothing to hinder you from being happy children of God, when carefully, habitually, diligently, you read the Word of God. Now, after we have added knowledge to virtue, it is said, "and to knowledge add temperance". This does not mean merely to avoid excess in eating and drinking; all this is implied; but it means more than this. It means self-control, that is, to seek to keep more and more under, all our natural, evil tendencies, such as passion, envy, pride, the love of money, the love of dress, the love of worldly pleasures and amusements; to keep under idleness, to aim at all that which glorifies God. O, beloved in Christ, are we doing this? Are we seeking to act more and more according to this-that we have self-control over our natural tendencies? In ourselves we are perfect weakness; we cannot do it, but we can cry to God that He would help us, and strengthen us to keep down more and more these natural tendencies, for if we indulge them it will prove a stumbling block to the unconverted. If we seek to keep under self-control, we not only glorify God, but strengthen the children: of God, and remove stumbling blocks.

Then to temperance we must add patience-that grace by which we meekly, submissively, without fretting, complaining, and much less murmuring, bear the afflictions of life. One says, "I am naturally impatient, and I cannot help it." This is a mistake, my brother and sister. Being tried, immediately cry to God. He will enable thee to keep under thy impatience.

The world is looking on, and by thy impatience thou art dishonouring and weakening the hands of thy brothers and sisters in Christ, while, on the other hand, thou art glorifying God by bearing the trials and afflictions of life. "All" these "things work together for good," and out of all these difficulties and trials God will bring blessing to thy soul. By thy impatience thou art dishonouring God, and by patiently bearing the trials of life thou art glorifying God.

Then to patience we are to seek to add godliness. Godliness-that is the grace by which we do what we do, to the honour of God, in the sight of God, as looking to God for help and strength, so that, more and more, we get into this state of heart. "Whether we eat or drink, we do it to the glory of God." If we have a morsel of meat, or drink of water, we do it to the glory of God. Ah! this grace. O for this grace! It is the kind of grace that the Blessed One had, who had it for His meat and drink, to do it to the glory of His Father. Although we do not compare ourselves with Christ, as if we were anything like Him, yet what God did for Him, He is willing to do for us. He is willing to "strengthen us with might, by His Spirit in the inner man."

Then to godliness we ate to add brotherly kindness-the love of the brethren, the children of God, not because they are our relatives, not to love them because they are in the same position in life, not to love them because they are of the same education, not because they are of the same church to which we belong, but to love them because they are believers in the Lord Jesus Christ. The more we do this, the more we glorify God. All the believers in Christ should love one another. No distinction between rich and poor, learned and illiterate, whether they belong to of the same church, or to another church-we are to love one another because we belong to Christ. Is it this after which we aim, my beloved friends? This is the very reason why I came here. I love the beloved brethren and sisters in Philip Street Baptist Chapel. I love all who love the Lord Jesus Christ, and for seventeen years, in which I was almost always travelling about in all parts of the earth-in Europe, and all over Europe repeatedly, in America, in Africa, in Asia, in India, all over India repeatedly, and in China and Japan, and in the six colonies of Australia-wherever I went I preached in the Church of England, amongst the Congregationalists, amongst the Baptists, amongst the Methodists, among all denominations, and I preached provided they loved the Lord Jesus Christ. I would not preach in Socinian chapels, lest it should be supposed I did not care about the divinity of the Lord Jesus Christ. I would not preach in the Roman Catholic churches and chapels, lest it should be supposed I was an admirer of the Pope. Wherever the foundation of our "most holy faith" was laid, there I preached.

Now, let us aim increasingly, beloved brethren, after this-that we love all who love our Lord Jesus Christ.

Then to this brotherly kindness we should add love. To love those who do not love us, to love those who are not believers in the Lord Jesus Christ, and our very enemies, because the more we have of this love, the more we have of God, for it is expressly said that" love is of God," and the more we are like God, the more we love.

What will be the result of all this? We see in the next two verses. "For if these things be in you, and abound, they make you that ye shall neither be barren nor unfruitful in the knowledge of our Lord Jesus Christ. But he that lacketh these things is blind, and cannot see afar off, and hath forgotten that he was purged from his old sins."

No one will be an idler in the Church of God who aims at thus building up himself on his most holy faith. He will care to win souls for Christ in one way of another, nor be "unfruitful in the knowledge of our

Lord Jesus Christ." He will live to God's honour and glory. "He that lacketh these things is blind." Spiritual dimness of sight is the result of this, if we do not seek "to build up ourselves on our most holy faith."

Again and again in our day, when persons are brought into spiritual difficulties, they know not how to act, because they have been so little acquainted with God and His ways. "They do not build up themselves." We should know how to act in difficulties, and this will be the case if we seek to build up ourselves; and if we do not know how to act in difficulties, the remedy is to aim at this-that we build up ourselves. And another boon we need continually in our day-people do not know whether their sins are forgiven or not. How comes this, if they are believers in Christ? Because they do not build up themselves in their most holy faith. They do not know how they stand before God, and that their sins are forgiven. "Wherefore the rather, brethren, give diligence to make your calling and election sure." Here is another blessing-the result of building up ourselves on our most holy faith. We know we have been called out of the world, that we are on the road to heaven, and when this life is over, we shall enter into everlasting life. This is the result of building up ourselves. And another blessing will result. We are thus "kept from falling"-that is, a person who is seeking to build up himself on his most holy faith will not bring disgrace on the name of the Lord. He will not be found a drunkard, he will not abscond with large sums of money in his pocket. None of these things occur on the part of those who profess to be disciples of the Lord Jesus Christ, and build themselves up on their most holy faith.

And one more blessing in the next verse. "For so an entrance shall be ministered unto you abundantly into the everlasting kingdom of our Lord and Saviour Jesus Christ" We should desire to enter the haven like a vessel, under full sail, enters the harbour. Do you think of this?

It has been thousands of times my prayer that my last days may be my best, and that I may, like a vessel under full sail, enter the haven. O, my beloved brethren and sisters in Christ, should this not be yet the aim of all of you? Ask God to bring you to this mind, that you, in the remainder of your life, may glorify and love God, and that at last, like a vessel under full sail, you may enter the haven of eternal love and blessedness. God grant it, for Christ's sake!

Chapter 20: "Behold! What Manner of Love."

A Sermon preached at Bethesda Chapel, Great George Street, Bristol, on Sunday Evening, April 11th, 1897 ·

1 John 3:1-3

BECAUSE WE NEED again and again to be reminded of the truth contained in these verses, God directs our especial attention to this little portion by prefixing the word, "Behold!" As if He meant to say," My dear children, the whole of the revealed will of God, the whole of the Holy Scriptures, which I put into your hands, is of importance to be considered, to be pondered and to be read from time to time; but there are certain portions which, by reason of your spiritual infirmity and by reason of the difficulties in which you find ourselves spiritually whilst passing through this vale of tears, you need especially to read from time to time, you need especially to ponder from time to time; and therefore, by reason of your weakness, I direct your attention to such portions."

Now, then, let us ponder, particularly ponder, the truth contained in this little statement made in these three verses. "Behold!" "Look at it carefully, ponder it, pray over it again and again, lay it to heart yet more and more than, up to the present, you have been doing," our Father would say to us! "What manner of love the Father hath bestowed on us, that we should be called the sons of God." That is the especial point to which, in the first place, our attention is directed. If God had forgiven us, so that punishment had not come on us on account of our numberless transgressions, and had done no more, this would have been wondrous grace; but He has done far, *far*, FAR more than this. And therefore it is stated, "What manner of love." The greatness of it, the exceeding greatness of it, the peculiarity of it, that not only has the Lord passed by our numberless transgressions, and forgiven everyone of them, so that we shall not be dealt with according to the thousandth part of the sins of which we have been guilty-nay, not concerning one single sin even, in action, in word, or in thought-but that He makes us His own children, takes us into the Heavenly Family. We, who are by nature rebels against Him, and despise His love, and care not in the least about Him, and manifest this entire dislike and disregard of God day by day by going our own way, doing the things which are hateful to Him-we are not only forgiven, not only shall not be punished for one single sin, out of the many ten thousands of sins of which we have been guilty, in action, or word, or thought, or feeling, or desire, or inclination, but are made His own children, taken into His family, and that not merely in name, but in reality. By the power of the Holy Spirit, through belief in the Gospel, He regenerates us, makes us a new creation in Christ, makes us His very own children. Not merely calls us so, but makes us His very own children. Gives us spiritual life, heavenly life, and thus makes us His very own children.

That is the wondrous grace which we should ponder. That is what God calls upon us to ponder, not to pass by lightly, not to think little about, but to think very, very, very much of, and never let pass out of our mind till we at last get home to glory! This is the "manner of love," the kind of love which "the rather hath bestowed upon us." O Lord! help us to ponder it a thousand times more than as yet we have pondered it. O Lord! help us, by the power of Thy Holy Spirit, to lay it to heart a thousand times more than as yet we have laid it to heart; and grant that, through the consideration of it, through praying over it, through laying it far more abundantly to heart than we have hitherto done, our hearts may be filled with love to Thee and with gratitude in a way in which as yet has not been the case! O grant it to be even so, for Jesus Christ's sake, we entreat Thee.

"Behold, what manner of love the Father hath bestowed upon us." Now, here is a good practical point "Bestowed upon us"; and to be able to say, "Bestowed upon me." That is what I, by the grace of God, am able to say. That is what, by the grace of God, many scores here present are able to say. But is everyone able to say it? This is what I desire, this is what I pray that God would grant to everyone here present, that they shall each be able to say, "Hath bestowed on me." O how happy this would make us, how heavenly-minded it would make us, how dead to the world it would make us! And in a little degree it would make us more Christ-like than as yet we have been! "Bestowed upon us." That we sinners, such as we are, rebellious sinners, as we are by nature, should be called the sons of God-more literally and correctly the children of God, for it is a blessing bestowed not merely upon male believers, but on female believers, upon all who love the Lord Jesus, and trust in Him for the salvation of their souls! Therefore, that we should be called the children of God. O precious! unspeakably blessed this, that we belong to the Heavenly Family!

By nature every one of us are just as the Jews were, to whom the Lord Jesus said on one occasion, "Your father is the devil"-"for his works you do; you act according to his mind, you act according to your father the devil." Now, this was not merely true about the Israelites, to whom the Lord was speaking; but it is true regarding us, as we are not believers in the Lord Jesus. We may call ourselves children of God, and we may call God our Father, but it is not true so long as we are not trusting in the Lord Jesus Christ for the salvation of our souls; the moment, however, we believe in the Lord Jesus Christ, however long, however much we have lived in sin, and however varied our sins, however great they may have been, all is forgiven, we are regenerated through the reception of the Gospel, born again, and verily then are the children of God, and belong to the Heavenly Family!

Then the Holy Ghost by the Apostle adds, "Therefore the world knows us not because it knew Him not." The children are not known because the Father is not known. As long as persons are not believers in the Lord Jesus Christ, they do not know the children of God as children of God! They may know their name, they may know their occupation, they may know where they live, how they are dressed, and such like things which belong to the outward man, and which belong to this present time; but, in so far as they are the children of God, those who themselves are unconverted know not the believers in Jesus, and the reason is given to us here, "Because they know not the Father" of the children. They know not God Almighty and the Lord Jesus Christ, and therefore they do not really and truly know the children of God as children of God. The divine life cannot be discerned by the ungodly.

"Beloved, now are we the sons of God"; "Beloved, now we are the children of God,"-for the same alteration is here to be made. "Now!" This little word, "now," is especially to be considered, to be laid hold of, and to be greatly pondered. It means this, while yet in the body-that is, while still in weakness, beset with many infirmities in many regards, and very ignorant in that state of weakness and helplessness in which to a greater or less degree are all true believers in the Lord Jesus Christ-nevertheless we are children of God; for though we are not all like John, who wrote this Epistle, or like Paul, or like Peter, yet, notwithstanding all our many infirmities and weaknesses and failures and shortcomings, as assuredly as we put our trust in the Lord Jesus Christ for the salvation of our souls, we are already, even while yet in the body, really and truly the children of God! A precious truth is this! And on this little word, "now," we have to lay hold by faith, to ponder it in our hearts again and again and again, and not to let it go, nor to suppose that we only become children of God when we die, or when the Lord Jesus Christ comes again.

Nay, now already are we the children of God. This, as you all at once see, even the youngest of the believers, implies that we have a Father in heaven, and that this our Father in heaven is none other than God Almighty-the God who can do everything, to Whom nothing is impossible. See how precious this is. Our Father can do everything! Therefore, He is infinitely wise; He is infinitely rich, He is infinitely mighty; and His heart is full of infinite love to the weakest and feeblest of the children of God. Therefore, suppose I have pain as to the body, let me go to my Heavenly Father, and speak in all child-like simplicity about it, and ask Him, if it be for His glory and for my real good, and profit, and blessing, that He would graciously be pleased either to entirely remove or else to mitigate the pain, or, while it is necessary that it should last, that He would be pleased to sustain me under it that I may not be overcome by it, and especially that I may not fret, and complain, and murmur, but take it out of His loving hand as a blessing bestowed upon me, which in the end must prove good for me. If we are in family trial, we should say to ourselves, "This family trial is not only very heavy for me to bear, but it will prove too much if I myself have to bear it; I will commit the matter into the hands of my Heavenly Father, and ask Him that He would be graciously pleased to remove the trial, if it be for His honour and glory and for my real blessing." He is able to do it, for He can do everything, and He has proved the depth of His love in not sparing His only-begotten Son, but delivering Him up for us all.

Then, again, persons in places, or in businesses, or carrying on a profession, find difficulties connected with their trade, connected with their business, connected with their profession. Now, the great point is not to carry the burden ourselves, but to cast it upon the Lord. He is willing to sustain us, willing to help us; and, in doing so, we pass peacefully and quietly through life, we are not inclined to fret, to complain, to murmur, and to be dissatisfied with the dealings of God with us, if we cast the burden upon Him, and not attempt to carry it ourselves!. And this is just what we should do; and this is just one of the many reasons why it is stated here by the Holy Spirit, "Now are we the children of God "-that is, while yet in the body, while yet surrounded by trial and difficulty, while yet finding that conflict is more or less our lot. O this little precious word, "NOW." It contains a vast deal of deeply instructive, instructing truth.

Again, we have now the spiritual conflict, our natural evil tendencies still are in us, though we are regenerated. The old nature is not removed; the old nature remains in us, just as it was before our faith in the Lord Jesus Christ. It is true we are regenerated, we are born again; it is true we have spiritual life-but it is also true that the old nature is not dead; the old nature still is in us, and can only be kept down by prayer and meditation and pondering the Word of God, and exercising faith continually. And therefore when trials come with regard to the old, evil, corrupt nature in us, we should spread the matter in all simplicity before God, and say, "My Heavenly Father, I have no strength in myself; but there is almighty power with Thee, and Thine heart is full of love to me, and Thou hast proved Thy wondrous love to me by bringing me to Jesus, and by giving Jesus for me, a poor, miserable, guilty sinner. Now help me in this my spiritual conflict. O let me not be overpowered by this subtlety of the devil, and on account of my spiritual weakness. O help me! help me! help me!" What shall we find? The Lord is willing to help us! The Lord is willing to help us!!

I assure my young brethren and sisters in Christ how He has helped me, now for seventy-one years and five months, times without number, and particularly at the beginning of the divine life in me. On account of the evil habits that I had contracted as an unconverted young man, the ungodly way in which I had been living up to the end of the twentieth year of my life, I found it extremely difficult, though really a child of God and though hating sin and loving holiness, to overcome those evil tendencies which I had contracted.

The appearance was, "O it will never be different, and my prayer will never be answered." But by the grace of God I have rolled my burden on Him, and come to Him again and again. Thus by little and little it came about-and it was by little and little only; it took some time-that these natural evil tendencies were overcome, and God helped me. I mention this particularly for the comfort and encouragement of young, recently converted believers in Christ not to despair, but to expect help from God, for He is able and willing to help them. Never, never, so long as we go to the Lord in our weakness and helplessness, shall we be overpowered; and just because we are the children of God now, therefore the glory will be our portion at last.

It is not that we become children of God when this life is over; nay, while we are y e body, while we are yet here on earth, while we are yet in great weakness and helplessness and great ignorance concerning many things, and while the devil has power over us, while he is not yet cast into the bottomless pit-even now we are the children of God, and shall have help from God just as we need. O how comforting is this word. Therefore let us continually ponder it, and not lose sight of it.

"Beloved now"-in weakness; "now," while the devil has yet so much power; "now," while in such great ignorance-"are we the children of God, and it doth not yet appear what we shall be." Though we are now children of God, and, as such, have many privileges and may go continually to God for counsel, for advice, for help, for strength, for deliverance out of difficulties, for being supplied temporally and spiritually according to our need, yet with all this, great as the privileges are which already we enjoy, they are but little in comparison with what we shall have hereafter. Therefore, we have to ponder also this, that while, on one hand, this word "now" should never be lost sight of, yet on the other hand we should not forget what is written here, "It doth not yet appear what we shall be."

And what is it that will appear hereafter? What is it that I, poor, worthless worm that I am, shall have hereafter? What is it that I, an ignorant one, shall know hereafter? What is it that in me, a weak one, and an erring one, and a falling one, shall be found hereafter? O this is a deeply important thought. "It doth not yet appear what we shall be"-it is not yet manifested what we shall be. O how will it be as to the body? How will it be as to the soul? How will it be as to our knowledge? How will it be as to our spiritual power? How will it be as to our service for the Lord? O how will it be in every way? An eternal blessing shall be granted to us, henceforth, for ever!

"It doth not yet appear what we shall be, but we know that, when He shall appear, we shall be like Him, for we shall see Him as He is." When Jesus shall appear we shall be like Him-like Him as to His .glorified body, which He has had since His resurrection. Now, any of us who are often in pain as to the body, or finding their weakness and infirmity ever reminding them of their not yet being at home, and not yet having obtained the glorified body, O how precious the consideration that there is a day coming when there will not be found the least particle of uneasiness, nor of pain and suffering and weakness and helplessness, for we shall have a glorified body, exactly such a body as the Lord Jesus Christ has had since His own resurrection. A precious, bright, glorious prospect is this!

And in this body, because it will be such a body as the Lord Jesus Christ has had since His resurrection, we shall know nothing of weariness. At present, we may be able joyfully and gladly to work eight, ten, or twelve hours, sometimes fourteen, or even sixteen hours a day, but at last the weakness comes by reason of yet being in the body of humiliation, and not in the glorified body. But, then, there will be four and twenty hours' work hereafter, and the next day the same, and the next day the same; and thus seven times four and twenty hours every week the ability to work; and thirty days every month the whole day able to work. And thus it will go on, month after month, year after year, one hundred years after the other, one thousand years after the other, one million years after the other, and so throughout eternity. Work, work, work! Constant work to the glory of God in this our glorified body! O what bright, blessed, glorious prospects are these, if the heart enter into them. O how we are gladdened by the consideration of working throughout eternity for God without the least particle of weakness, weariness, and suffering!

But this is only one part of it. The other part is this. We shall be perfectly holy as the Lord Jesus Christ was during the thirty-three years and a half that He was on earth! Never a particle of wrong found in anything that He did, never a particle contrary to the mind of God in anything that He said; never a particle found in all His thoughts, in all His desires, in all His wishes, contrary to the mind of God. Perfectly in conformity to the mind of God everything was found during the whole time that the blessed Saviour was here on earth! And thus it will be with us. We weak ones, feeble ones, shall not be always weak ones, feeble ones, but holy ones, spotless ones, pure ones, lovely ones. Yes, lovely ones! O how lovely! Because the comeliness of Christ is put on us! O how precious these words are; and O, if we bore them more in mind, if we entered into them, how the heart would be full of peace and joy all the day long and every day.

Now, it is on account of this that the statement is made, "It doth not yet appear what we shall be; but we know that, when He shall appear, we shall be like Him." We shall be like Him! Notice the reason why! "We shall be like Him, for we shall see Him as He is!" More correctly, "For we shall see Him even as He is." That is, we shall perfectly know the Lord Jesus Christ: in all His work and all His offices, not merely know Him as our Judge. In that way the ungodly will have to become acquainted with Him. Every human being, if they are not believers in Christ, will know Him as their Judge, but we shall know Him as our Saviour, as our Brother, as our Friend, as our Husband, as our Bridegroom. In every one of the offices which He sustains for the benefit of the Church of God we shall know Him; and, just in proportion as we know the Lord now, we are conformed to Him, we become more and more like Him, even while we are yet in the body. The more acquainted we are with the Lord Jesus Christ, the more are we like Him; and then in the glory we shall know perfectly that Blessed One, and we shall perfectly be like Him! What a bright and blessed prospect this is! So that not only without weakness and weariness, pain and suffering, will our service be throughout all eternity, but completely according to the mind of God, completely in the same spirit in which the Lord Jesus Christ was working while in the body here on earth! Precious, bright, glorious prospects are ours! It is just because the world is so ignorant, so completely ignorant, about all the glorious things which are the portion of the believer in Christ that they care not about the things of God; for were it known what really is the blessed position and portion of a child of God, everybody would seek to know Him, everybody would care about Him, everybody would believe on Him.

Now the last point, "And every man that hath this hope in Him purifieth himself, even as He is pure." First of all, as to the somewhat more correct literal meaning, "Every man"-that is, "everyone"-"that hath this hope in Him." The meaning is not, "Has this hope in himself." That is not the meaning of it; but "has this hope regarding the Lord Jesus Christ," that, through faith in Him, he will be perfectly like Christ in heaven. "Everyone that hath this hope in Him, or regarding Him, purifieth himself, even as He is pure." That is, as in every way truth has the tendency to increase holiness, so here we repeat again the statement. Whosoever has this hope regarding the Lord Jesus, to be made like Him in body and soul; everyone who has this hope regarding Him purifieth himself. It has a tendency to make us increasingly holy, for just as we become acquainted with Christ, and see what God has given us in Him, the more we know of this clearly, distinctly, minutely, and the more fully is holiness increased in us, so that we shall be satisfied with nothing short of this, that we may continually become more and more Christ-like.

We do not attain to it to the full while we are in the body; yet this will be our aim more and more, more and more, more and more to be like Christ. We are not satisfied with this, that we have power over our natural, gross sins; we are not satisfied with this, but only that in spirit, in mind, more and more, we are Christ-like, gentle and loving. O how increasingly we seek to attain to this; earnestly desiring it more and more; in every way seeking to become like Christ. And though to the full it will never be attained to while in the body, yet it is impossible to say to what a degree we may, even while in the body, become Christ-like.

Now, let this be the great lesson that we learn this evening, that because we are now already children of God, blessing, wonderful blessing, is to be obtained from our Heavenly Father; and that, by reason of the prospect we have before us, it is impossible to say to what a degree we may not become Christ-like. Now, will you who are not believers in Christ always continue in the way in which you have been going on hitherto? Shall there be no alteration? If you continue on the broad way, final destruction will be your portion! Do you long to spend a happy eternity together with the Lord in heaven? O what delight it will be to many at the last to see not one of all who are present here lacking in heaven!

This is a personal interest I have in your spiritual welfare, and out of love to your soul, that I long to meet you in heaven; and O how it would increase our joy and delight in heaven at last to find not one lacking, to find that this our little meditation on the evening of the 11th of April, 1897, was not in vain. O how precious to find it thus at the last! And now, is there anyone present who says, "I will yet have the world; I will yet seek to enjoy the world?" You will not be happy by this determination; be quite sure of that. O I tried your ways for twenty years and five weeks, and all that ever I got was disappointment and increased guilt on the conscience. But when I found Jesus there came real happiness. O such happiness as I cannot describe. That was in the beginning of November, 1825, and I have felt it ever since-only with this difference, that the happiness increased more and more, more and more. And that is what God is willing to give to you; for I suppose there is not a greater sinner here present than I was, though but twenty years of age, yet God bestowed this wondrous blessing on me; and what He did for me, and what He did for Paul, and what He did for other sinners, He is willing to do for anyone else.

Therefore, O let it be Christ whom you choose, and not the world any longer; for the world never will prove real, but, if continued in, will bring damnation, and only damnation. God grant His blessing, for Jesus Christ's sake.

END

For hundreds of other excellent titles see:

www.Classic*Christian*Ebooks.com

Also available by George Muller:

Answers to Prayer
Counsel to Christians
Biography of George Muller (by A. T. Pierson)
Preaching Tours and Missionary Labours of George Muller
George Muller's Autobiography ("The Life of Trust")
George Muller: Ten Years After